Advance Praise

———— ◆ ————

"One of the paradoxes of leadership in the Episcopal Church is that while we have ordained women for more than a generation, we still continue to frame successful pastoral leadership in ways which reinforce patriarchal patterns. While many claim to want new styles of leadership and more diverse clergy leadership, many young women and others who do not fit the traditional mold, find the journey to, and realities of, clergy leadership roles to be isolating, frustrating and diminishing. This bold and refreshing reflection on vocation and leadership offers deep insights on the challenges for young women in the church today and gives all concerned with formation and ministry suggestions for the way forward."

~   The Rev. Dr. Sheryl A. Kujawa-Holbrook, Ed.D, Ph.D, Claremont School of Theology, author of *God Beyond Borders, Injustice and the Care of Souls* and *A House of Prayer for All Peoples*

"The Rev. Dr. Sara Shisler Goff is a woman who knows the struggles of wanting to minister in the midst of a patriarchal church and she has written a book to help not just her clergy sisters, but all those who desire the full life of God in their ministry. At its core this book is a call to explore our relationships with all that is: cosmos, earth, others, patriarchy, sexua_____ ourselves.

Shisler Goff is wise enough to know that authentic lives spring from our ability to be honest with ourselves, to know, intimately, our feelings and how this affects every aspect of our lives. This means we cannot deceive ourselves but must live our most honest lives if we hope to have an effective and free ministry. In self-revealing, vulnerable risks, Shisler Goff takes her readers on a journey of exercises and insights that will enable one to cast off the weights that imprison women (and men) in ministry. Her challenge to take stock of our relationship to God and others places us in the space of realizing how sidetracked we become from the things that truly matter. Most helpful is when she looks at the way we sabotage ourselves by self-hate and self-criticism, and the piling on that takes place when congregations try to exploit this weakness. The benefit of Shisler Goff's book is that it gives the reader very pragmatic exercises that can be done with small groups or oneself to move to places of freedom found in self-worth. Her journey to wholeness in her ministry allows her readers to examine and explore the places within themselves that need tending and care in order to be a fierce pastoral presence in a broken world."

~ Jeffrey C. Pugh, Professor Emeritus, Elon University, author of *Religionless Christianity: Dietrich Bonhoeffer in Troubled Times* and *The Matrix of Faith: Reclaiming a Christian Vision*

"When some years ago the Southern Baptists made official what had long been a widespread practice, prohibiting women from serving as pastors, I remember thinking, "Oh God, what a loss to those congregations!" In The Art of

Feminine Spiritual Leadership, the Rev. Sara Shisler Goff shows us so much of the fullness of what those Baptists and others have shunned while clinging to an outmoded and ultimately self-limiting patriarchal model of ministry. In the process she also effectively addresses many of the major difficulties faced by women ministers in a religious institution and a society all too often still caught in that patriarchal clench. Rev. Shisler Goff's finger is firmly on the pulse of the broader contemporary Church, and her keen insights into the nature and promise of empathetic and empowered ministry are timed perfectly for this moment of generational change that could well move the Church forward toward greater inclusivity and effectiveness in its mission. Yet this is not just a women's book. Regardless of gender orientation, pastors and other church leaders will find in these pages tools aplenty for their work, along with clarity for their confusion and inspiration to light the way forward. All of us owe The Rev. Dr. Shisler Goff a debt of gratitude for finding the courage and fortitude to transform her own frustrations into a readable, hands-on guide to becoming "'the leader you were born to be.'"

~   L.D. Russell, author of *Godspeed: Racing Is My Religion*

"In *The Art of Feminine Spiritual Leadership*, the Rev. Dr. Sara Shisler Goff offers an exciting opportunity for clergy, parishioners and the wider Church to expand our vision for and embodiment of spiritual leadership. Celebrating and cultivating "Feminine Spiritual Leadership," as defined by Shisler Goff, could contribute to a 21st century reformation or awakening of the Church - theologically, spiritually, and organizationally. As Shisler Goff makes clear, feminine spiritual leadership is not to be placed in opposition to current dominant, masculine spiritual leadership. Rather, Shisler Goff invites all people to imagine and re-form what spiritual leadership means, individually and collectively. I recommend this book for all people in ministry - for women clergy fed up with the institutional church, for male and non-binary clergy seeking to expand their own understanding and embodiment of spiritual leadership, for lay and ordained leaders on Discernment Committees, Commissions on Ministry, Bishop's Nominating Committees, and anyone else committed to the transformation of our Church and to being and acting as the Body of Christ in this world."

~   The Rev. Dr. Teresa Danieley, priest, Episcopal Diocese of Missouri, and Champions Organizer, Missouri Jobs with Justice

"Finally, a book on leadership that understands how femininity is a power! It isn't something to be overcome or something to hide. It isn't something that keeps you out of boardrooms or pulpits, but something that our world needs in order to address all the challenges we face in our personal lives, the organizations for which we work, and in our communities."

~   Ann Phelps, vocalist, liturgist, theologian and co-founder of the *Theodicy Jazz Collective*

"Bold. Brave and intimate, Sara Shisler Goff takes us into the depths of her journey and the real struggles of what it means to be a woman in the church. In her straight talking, tell-it-like it-is style, she gives you powerful tools and the confidence to own your power and your softness, just as you are. If you are a woman who longs to access the depths of your desires and are ready to hear your own calling, this book is for you."

~   Stephanie Redlener, Leadership coach and organizational consultant, founder of *Lioness,* a leadership and change agency for women rising

"Sara's book has helped me to name some of the frustration that I am facing in my ministry, but even more importantly, some of the JOYS! Reading this book will leave you feeling refreshed and hopeful for the life of the church and the need for women's wisdom within it. Thank you for this resource."

~   The Rev. Dr. Hillary Raining, author of *Faith with a Twist: A 30-Day Journey into Christian Yoga* and *Joy in Confession: Reclaiming Sacramental Reconciliation*

"I'm thrilled to be reading this book, written with passion and compassion for women unabashedly taking on roles of leadership, just as they are. The Rev. Dr. Shisler Goff affirms the strengths of her readers, grounded in the work of reflection, spiritual practice and getting real about the power that female leaders can harness when we live into it fully. I'm excited to see a generation of female clergy empowered and unleashed by this inspiring and uplifting volume. Ladies, let's do this!"

~ The Rev. Mary Catherine Young, Episcopal chaplain, New York University

The
ART *of* Feminine
SPIRITUAL
LEADERSHIP

Be a Badass Priest and
Create a Ministry You Love

THE REV. DR. SARA SHISLER GOFF

Difference Press

McLean, Virginia, USA

Published 2019

ISBN: 978-1-68309-231-5

DISCLAIMER

Cover Design: Jennifer Stimson

Editing: Bethany Davis

For Heather.

Table of Contents

Foreword   xix

Introduction   xxv

CHAPTER 1

Ministry Was Not Supposed to Be like This   35

CHAPTER 2

The Bridge: Getting from Here to There   47

CHAPTER 3

Right Where You Are   57

CHAPTER 4

Your Relationship with Your Self   75

CHAPTER 5

Your Relationship with God   87

CHAPTER 6

Your Relationships with Others   107

CHAPTER 7

Your Relationship with All of Creation
/The Cosmos   123

CHAPTER 8

Feeling Is Your Superpower   137

CHAPTER 9

The Wisdom of Your Body   155

CHAPTER 10

The Power of Pleasure   165

CHAPTER 11

We Are Not Supposed to Do This Alone   179

CONCLUSION

Becoming the Person You Are Meant to Be   193

Further Reading   197
Acknowledgments   198
About the Author   199
About Difference Press   200
Other Books by Difference Press   202
Thank You!   203

Foreword

Being a leader is not easy. Being a courageous leader of integrity is harder, still. Being a queer female leader of a patriarchal religious organization? Challenging as f*ck. Might as well hang your butt in the breeze, place a target on it and pass out darts.

Not too different from how Jesus must have felt, pretty much on the daily, as he did his part in opening a portal for our culture to advance.

The beauty, brilliance and heartbreak of Sara Shisler Goff's book is having a front pew seat to her journey to evolve a hierarchical church with a not yet resolved history of sexism, racism and homophobia. The triumph is witnessing the power of feminine spiritual leadership—and Sara's love—to take her church to its next evolutionary level.

This book is an important read, not only for all women in the clergy, but for all humans who have a call to lead. Sara's book is a course on feminine spiritual leadership, which is about leading from a place of pleasure, desire and abundance. And faith.

If you are reading this book, I would imagine you have a desire that is pressing on you, preoccupying you, leaning on you. But, like many women, the moment you have a desire is the very moment you get flooded with doubt. You might feel you don't have enough experience or knowledge to do the thing you desire. You might be overwhelmed by all that you don't know. You might not believe anyone will follow you. There are so many reasons why women choose to stay stuck in our doubts rather than choose to say "yes" to the still, small voice of our deepest calling.

You, sister, need to know—and choose to believe—that you are resourceful, capable and powerful beyond your own understanding of yourself. You *are* a leader. And you can lead yourself from here to whatever it is you desire. How? By practicing the art of feminine spiritual leadership.

In this book, Sara Shisler Goff outlines what feminine spiritual leadership looks like. Here are just a few of my favorites:

- Feminine spiritual leadership starts with longing.
- Feminine spiritual leadership is self-aware.
- Feminine spiritual leadership walks to the edge of what is known and jumps off.
- Feminine spiritual leadership walks the talk.
- Feminine spiritual leadership is comfortable with the uncomfortable.
- Feminine spiritual leadership is all the things you already are, that you just need to remember and give yourself permission be.
- Feminine spiritual leadership is done in sisterhood.

If your leadership style (and I don't care who you are, you have one) skews more feminine, in this culture, that may lead you to believe you don't have what it takes to do what you want to do. That is a lie. All you need to be a bad*ss priest and create a ministry you love is desire and your whole self.

See, we have been taught, by the patriarchy, to regard what is feminine as not sacred, not powerful, not useful, not glorious. We have been trained to see our gifts as liabilities, flaws, faults, failure; as wrong.

As Sara will teach you, a woman needs tools to find her way back to herself. And it is nearly impossible to do, when you are alone. We need sisterhood. We need other women. Women at our side not only when things are great, but women who, when we are off track, are right there to remind us we are more than this. We need a community, a congregation, a choir to sing with.

When Sara signed up to work with me in my advanced course, she had already begun her journey, but she still wanted more. She wanted to go deeper into sisterhood—she knew she needed a community of women to take her even higher—to discern and live into her best life. She wanted to go deeper into her grief, anger and fear. She wanted to get to the roots of her dark emotions and learn to accept them, love them and live her full truth. But she had 35 years of experience with shoving her feelings down, lowering her expectations of sisterhood and motherhood, swallowing her truth. She was used to being in pain.

When I met Sara, I could see she was searching for something. I had the sense that she was searching not just for her own benefit, but for her sisters who were not yet in the room with us. Within her quest to heal herself is a deeper quest—she desires to heal the church and heal the world.

In my work with women at The School of Womanly Arts, I have learned that, as women, we are given no language to describe that which is most essentially *us*—we have no words to describe feminine power, because "feminine" and "power" have been defined by the patriarchy to exist in complete opposition to one another.

My father used to read to us from the Bible every Friday night. "In the beginning was the Word." When there is no word, there is no beginning. We need words to locate and own our power as women.

In this book, Sara offers her words, her story of how she went from barely being able to recognize her longings, to letting go of anyone else's dream for her life and choosing to own her worth and herself. Not only did this take her on an epic journey of self-discovery, it completely transformed her ministry and her life. Here she introduces tools she has both collected and created along her path and offers them to you, so you can take them and begin to create a passion-filled, powerful life and vocation for yourself.

For Sara, there is an inherent connection between loving herself and loving God. My wish for you—and for all women—is to find that magnificent connection, too. May this book be that beginning.

Regena Thomashauer
Founder, The School of Womanly Arts

Introduction

———————◆———————

*"There is a whisper we keep hearing; it is saying
we must build in us what we want to see built
in the world."*

— SONYA RENEE TAYLOR

When I first started writing this book, I had a picture in my mind of the person who would read it. She (yes, she was a she) was a minister in a Christian denomination like the Episcopal Church. She had been ordained for a decade or so and in that time she had experienced the typical highs and lows that come with a life of ministry. But there was more going on with her and in her than meets the eye. Perhaps her dissatisfaction ran deeper than she let on – maybe even to herself. She was finally admitting to herself just how frustrated she really was, and yet, at the same time, how hopeful....

If this sounds like you, welcome! I'm glad you are here. (If it does not sound like you, I'm still glad you are here and I trust you will still get something out of these pages). You, however, may not be glad you are here, because being here means you are, in some way, dissatisfied with your current ministry.

First, I want to tell you that you are not alone. You are indeed special, but not because you are struggling with your ministry. Every clergy person – especially every young, female clergyperson is currently experiencing some kind of struggle in her ministry. How do I know that? Because as much as the church has changed over the last few decades and as far as we have come in many areas, the main models of leadership continue to reflect masculine characteristics and to champion patriarchal values. Therefore, being a leader who identifies as a woman and with the feminine, means always going against the grain – and this means struggle.

Not that struggle is always bad. Tension is often where we grow! It can just be exhausting, especially given the isolating nature of many of our ministry contexts. In some way, we are all blazing our own trail, and as exciting and invigorating as that can be, it is also intense and laborious work. And, since we are all basically making it up as we go along, any doubts or misgivings that creep in have plenty of space to find a foothold and yell at us with all their might: "You don't know what you are doing! Who do you think you are? Do you really think that is going to work? What will people think of you? Don't get too big for your britches," or "cause too much of a stir," or "rock the boat," or "offend the wrong people," the list goes on. Our internal monologues alone are enough to keep us paralyzed, besides what anyone else might actually say to us out loud.

We knew the church was not perfect when we signed up for the priesthood (or to be a pastor or minister, depending on your context. For my purposes I'm going to refer to us all as "priests;" if you have a ministry you are a minister, ordained or not, so please consider yourself included. I really do believe in the "priesthood of all believers" and it is my book so I can do what I want!) But if you are anything like me, you still held out great hope that because the church was *the church* any efforts that focused on loving God and serving our neighbors would surely be supported. Turns out the church is full of human beings. As my wife likes to say, any institution that includes human beings is going to have its problems.

I could write an entire book on the failings of the church, and someday I probably will, even if only for my own catharsis. But this book is about you and me and our desire to stay *in* the church, no matter how angry it makes us and how frustrated we get, because we love God and we love God's people. Not to mention that whole "calling" thing. We did not choose this calling, we were chosen for it. We have been chosen because of who we are and who we have been created by God to be – all of us – lady bits included.

In my experience it is not just the "lady bits" that make the church nervous – it is the fact that women are leaders. In my denomination it has been forty years since eleven women went rogue and said, "Screw it. We know that we are called to the priesthood. Time's up, church." With the help of a few brave bishops, they were "irregularly" ordained and later, after much weeping and gnashing of teeth, their ordinations were accepted by the church.

Sometimes the church is not ready, but God is. When you know this but the church does not, it is a precarious position to find yourself in. But fear not, dear one, because it is also awesome, as evidenced by 95 percent of the stories in our biblical canon. If you can hang on for the ride, most of the time everyone else will come around.

I don't mean to make light of the resistance we face. I do hope to encourage you that at the end of the day, God is in charge no matter what, so all we can do is our best to be faithful. I have learned firsthand how difficult it can be to be faithful to God when the church is not there yet. I've also learned how miserable it is to choose the status quo over the prophetic now. God is redeeming us all, so keep breathing.

I know you deeply desire to become the priest God is calling you to be. Part of this means feeling a strong call to go deeper, do more, be bolder, speak up. I know you feel this calling in your bones and you can taste its sweetness on your tongue. I also know you don't know *exactly* what all this means or what it is going to look like or how it is going to happen ... yet. And that probably freaks you out a bit. But rest assured, *you do not need to know right now*. You are not *supposed* to know right now.

Every area in which you are struggling is a hint of where God is at work in your life, stirring sh*t up and getting you ready for what is next. Again, you don't need to know what is next. You just need to know that you *desire more*. You are ready to give more. You are ready to take your leadership to the next level and take the people you serve even higher.

But how to do you claim this power you are starting to feel, without turning into "one of those priests"? How do you maintain your integrity and stay honest about who you are – your shortcomings and weaknesses as well as your strengths and skills? How do you keep your ego in check *and* find the hutzpah to speak up when you know you have something important to say? How do you lead as your true, bad*ss self?

All very good questions, my dear, and in this book I desire to chew them over with you. I have been chewing on these questions for the past decade, searching for ways to reignite my passion for ministry that was there at the beginning and seeking ways to make the difference I was born to make in the church. Finding and creating my place in the church has been a struggle. I always knew, deep down, that the traditional models of ministry and priest-hood would never be a fit for me. But as I went through the process of discerning a call to the priesthood within the Episcopal Church, the message was pretty clear – I had to fit a certain mold, or fit it enough, to be accepted. I also think the experience of trying to fit and *not fitting* was part of my discernment. I had to experience the discomfort of not fitting to be 100 percent sure that if I wanted to be true to myself, I was going to have to make another way. And I had to fall more and more in love with the church – in love with God's people – to not simply throw in the towel when things got tough. And believe me, they got *really tough* at times. I know you know. I know you have been there, too.

Ultimately, I'm grateful that I don't fit. It is much more fun and life-giving to create something new than to go along with the status quo. Right now the church as a whole is being called to something new, but not everyone hears that call or is ready to accept it. But you are. Your ministry and, in a very real way, your life, depends on your answer to this radical call.

I know it is scary. But I am also here to tell you it is really, *really incredible.* Even the scary parts are incredible once you realize and come to believe that you were made for this. I already know it; in this book I hope to help you come to know it, too.

You are in for an amazing journey and I am honored to travel this leg of it with you. In this book, I will share tools and practices I have found helpful along the way and some lessons I have learned. My goal is that we can help each other not only to stick it out in the church, but to create thriving ministries where we feel fulfilled and validated in our callings. Because the church needs us, and we need the church.

Over the past decade I have been lucky enough to have been part of several amazing communities, some of which are affiliated with the church and some which are not. The tools I have been introduced to and the experiences I have had have been essential parts of my journey from trying to follow a more traditional priestly path and fit into some external standard of what a priest should be, to giving myself permission to be honest with myself about my longings for ministry and take the risk of believing in myself and my own worth enough to let go of what was to create what could be.

Part of my journey has been admitting to myself that the way I am a priest and the way I lead is different than the norm – i.e., the traditional, masculine model of priesthood. As crazy as it sounds, I had to go so far as to forgive myself for that before I could claim it as a good thing. This is no wonder, given that even the places in the church that have moved away from the traditional "father knows best" model of priest still struggle when their clergy and ministry leaders do things differently than they are used to. Part of this is how systems work and change and part of it is patriarchal and hierarchical ways of being that are deeply engrained in our DNA. We still have a lot to unlearn and you and I are not exempt from that unlearning process. We need to give ourselves time and space, resources and technology to unlearn the ways of being that are no longer necessary or useful and to take on the new mantles of awesomeness that are our birthright as female priests. This fun and at times arduous process involves excavating and exploring parts of ourselves we have buried, parts we didn't even know were there, parts that still have the training wheels on. I'm talking about those things that make us unique and special; what makes us ... *dunn dunn daaaa* *feminine.*

That's right, I said it. The word is in the title, so you should not be too surprised. Hopefully, you are even open to the idea that what is "feminine" and what is "spiritual" have something to do with "leadership." Spoiler alert. They do. They totally do. This book is about finding those things within ourselves, naming them, claiming them, and working them for all they are worth for the love of God.

So yes, I am going to argue in this book that there are advantages to embracing a feminine spiritual leadership style. It will look something like being your total, unashamed, bad*ss self. Radical, I know. But guess what? It works. Meaning, not only will you finally be able to stop pretending to be some other person's version of a priest, but you will tap back into the essence of your calling and let that power start coursing through your veins again.

See, it's starting right now. Can you feel it?

Now, if the transformation from hating your life to loving your ministry seems too good to be true, or at least, too good to ever happen to you, let me tell you more about my story thus far. Grab some tea – or wine – and settle in. The following is a true story. Here it comes: the good, the bad, and the ugly of my first few years in ministry.

CHAPTER 1

Ministry Was Not Supposed to Be like This

———— ◆ ————

"This is not the life I planned ... But it is the life that has turned out to be mine, and the central revelation in it for me – that the call to serve God is first and last the call to be fully human."

– BARBARA BROWN TAYLOR, *LEAVING CHURCH*

I Want You to Want Me

It was not supposed to be this way, and yet, deep down, I was not at all surprised. After only a few years into my ministry as an ordained priest in the Episcopal Church, I found myself in the same position as many of the young clergy women who had gone before me – thinking about leaving. I had been warned this might happen. Two weeks before I was ordained I went to a conference for young clergy women and someone quoted a statistic that said that something like 50 percent of women under 30 leave the ministry after less than five years. I have searched every inch of the internet looking for this statistic, but it is nowhere to be found (am I reading too much into this in thinking that the lack of statistics only supports the notion we are not being cared for or supported?).

While I can't cite the study, I can remember the effect it had on me. It broke my heart to know that untold numbers of women leave the ministry they have spent years training for, thousands of dollars paying for, and countless hours dreaming of. For many, the dream never comes true and the nightmare is too much to take. If women ministers only had to contend with being undervalued and under-paid, maybe it wouldn't be so bad – it would be just like any other job experience. But ministry was supposed to be different ... right?

At first, it is surprisingly hard to name exactly what I had hoped would be different and what was causing my under-lying sense of unhappiness and dissatisfaction. I just knew that I needed and wanted an experience of ministry that was different than the one I was having. When I began to "flesh out" this feeling, I realized what I wanted was for the church where I ministered and served to be more like the church *I needed and wanted to be a part of.* In other words, I wanted my church to be a place where my relationships with others were rooted and grounded in love.

I wanted to feel known and seen. I wanted to be under-stood and affirmed for who I was. I wanted honesty and transparency. I wanted open and honest communication. I wanted support and authenticity. I wanted genuine, shared leadership. I wanted to be able to be courageous and vul-nerable without the fear of retribution or the fear of being knocked down. I wanted all those things we *all* want in our church and in our workplace. But it was more than just wanting them, I wanted to know *why they were not there*. I'm not saying they were never there, but too often they were not and that was upsetting.

Is This All There Is?

I had hoped that in the church I would not encounter outright sexism, blatant homophobia, and thinly veiled racism. I had hoped that an institution based on the teachings of Jesus would at least try to follow them, you know, most of the time. At the very least, I hoped that when leaders in the church screwed up, *which we all do*, we would at least *attempt* to practice what we preach – when, not if, we fall into sin, we repent and ask for forgiveness.

That is what I hoped. Again, I'm not saying this never happened. There were many times when, by the abundant grace of God, we mere mortals were able to do the hard, self-aware work of admitting and confessing our wrongs, repenting and asking for forgiveness, and granting one another absolution. It's amazing how this church stuff really does work! But it only works when we work it. I was shocked by how often those charged with leading the church chose not to practice its tools. It is one thing to encounter human failings from time to time. It's another to feel like standard operating procedure goes against our espoused core beliefs.

It was kind of like training to become a lifeguard, finally becoming certified, and realizing that there were times when the other lifeguards were struggling to just ... swim.

Maybe they could swim well at one point, but all the things they did to keep themselves strong and in shape had been put on the back burner now that their job was to save other people. They knew where the life rafts were kept and they were even pretty good at tossing them out to people in need. But was their number one priority taking care of themselves so they could stay in good shape and ready to serve? Were they honest about the fact that some waves had the power to pull *even them* under the current? Many of them did, but some of them didn't. Let me be clear, the problem is not the struggle at times to swim–that is human–the problem is the status quo supporting a lack of self-awareness and the resulting dangers.

Be the Change You Wish to See in the Church

It took me years to get to the place where I could even accept that God was calling me toward ordination. I did not grow up wanting to be a priest. Ordination never even occurred to me until I was almost finished with college and God strategically and stealthily orchestrated the implosion of my carefully-laid post-graduation plans. When I first began to recognize within myself a call to ordination, I was thoroughly confused. I felt an intense and specific call to be a priest, but at that point, I could not see myself in any clergy I knew. I knew that female priests existed, in theory, but it was not until I went to seminary that I actually met a female priest. Looking back now, I do not underestimate the effect this had on my ability to imagine myself in the role of priest. Because I couldn't *see* myself in any of the ministers I knew, it was difficult to claim my calling.

This would be the first of many times I would feel a calling to an unseen and as yet unknown expression of my vocation. I would argue this is the blessing and the curse of being called to ministry during this time of great change and upheaval in the church. You and I do not have the luxury of pointing to anyone or anything outside ourselves and being able to say, "That. That is exactly who I want to be. That is exactly what I am called to do." That person, that embodied expression of our unique vocation *will not exist until it exists in us.* We have to be it to see it.

The good news is, whether we have consciously realized it or not, we have had lots of practice pushing beyond what we can imagine and stepping into the unknown. It is called being a human being. Even if we *think* our life's path has been laid out for us and we are simply following the pre-written script, we have still chosen to step into that script, each step of the way. The secret is, none of it is actually written, none of it was preordained, none of it had to happen – we chose it, we made it happen, we partic-ipated in creating the life we have lived. (Clearly, I am not a Calvinist.) We did not make it happen all on our own, God was and is always at work in and through us. And, we had to say yes to the calling.

Yes … And?

I wavered and wobbled and withheld my full "yes" to ordi-nation for nearly my entire time in seminary. I just could not run full-on into the arms of a hierarchical church with a history of sexism, racism, and homophobia. Even though the Episcopal Church (TEC) has made and is making great strides in acknowledging the sins of our past, it still feels a bit like the significant other who treats you badly, apologizes and promises never to scream at you in public again, but still says really mean and hurtful things to you when you are in private. The big, outward behaviors may have changed, but the power dynamics and ways of relating still remain unhealthy.

From the outset, I resisted willingly choosing to participate in a hierarchical structure of leadership and relationships. I resisted putting my fate, my livelihood, and a huge part of my sense of self in the hands of a fallible institution. I resisted placing myself under the direct authority of whichever Bishop happened to oversee the diocese in which I lived and worked. I resisted the requirement to defer so much of my own autonomy in order to "serve the church" – the church I loved but also knew very, very well was far from perfect.

I resisted ordination. And yet, I did ultimately choose to be ordained, because I believe I am called by God to be a priest. Somehow I managed to convince committee after committee of my calling, but what ultimately convinced *me* was the feeling I experienced in the core of my being when I finally said "Yes." I had a feeling, an actual physical feeling in my body that felt like an awareness of *rightness* and a tug toward my future. I felt it in my throat, chest, and stomach. It felt warm and stirring, like I wanted to throw up, but in a good way. I feel it again right now as I write these words. I feel it every time I think about my calling to the priesthood. This feeling of rightness is what ultimately won out and outweighed any "wrongness" I knew I could possibly, and would likely, encounter in my ministry. Ultimately, I choose to say yes to God, to my calling, to ordination, and to the institutional church because I said yes to being myself.

Little did I know that I would need to hold on to the "yes" to God and to my self for dear life when my "yes" to the church felt like it might kill me. Not literally. I don't believe the church has literally put my life in danger, but I am lucky that way. I know others who are female or queer or young or different who cannot say the same.

#SorryNotSorry

In my first years of ministry I quickly learned there were times when saying "yes" to God meant saying "no" to the institutional church. For example, I could not say "yes" to taking the "advice" of my Bishop when he "suggested" I not talk or write publicly about being bisexual because it might make some people uncomfortable about my being their priest and limit the churches where I could serve. I could not say "yes" to a parent's request that we not talk about sexuality in youth group because she did not think it was appropriate but rather something parents should choose to talk about with their children at home. I could not say "yes" to the request from whichever church leader instructed there be no celebration on the floor of General

Convention when the announcement came through that the Episcopal Church had decided to approve a trial liturgy for the blessing of same-sex marriages, because not everyone would be happy about this decision and we should not "rub our victory in their faces" (to paraphrase what we were instructed).

F*ck that. #sorrynotsorry. Your distress does not get to kill my joy. Your discomfort does not get to shut down conversations. Your disapproval does not get to silence my voice. Your dis-ease does not get to erase my existence. Not anymore. Not even in the name of your Jesus or "our church."

Realizing this has been hard, I'm not going to lie to you. I know you have been there in your own life and ministry where "doing the right thing" according to the institutional church and "doing the right thing" according to your truth, your understanding, and your knowledge of God's justice and love *are not the same thing.* It is heartbreaking, every time. And, at least in my experience, the more you are faced with this choice, two things can start to happen. Either you start to question your inherent connection to the divine and the sense of rightness you were once so sure about, or you choose to believe in it even more.

Living on the Edge

There have always been people, both clergy and non-clergy, on the edges of the church, calling on the institution to expand its understanding of who is lovable, what is holy, and how we can access the divine. St. Francis did it. Theresa of Avila did it. Pierre Telihard de Chardin did it. Letty Russell did it. Katie Cannon did it. The truth is, *all women have done this,* by necessity and by dint of our circumstances – living in a patriarchal world culture (PWC). The church has, unfortunately, not set itself up as an alternative to patriarchy. Other than small patches of time and space, the church has been just as patriarchal as the rest of the world.

While you probably feel an intuitive sense of recognition when I mention living in the patriarchal world culture, have you ever taken time to unpack its effect on your life? Maybe you took a women's studies class in college. Maybe you are a part of a group of women who have created a safe space for yourselves to share your stories. These kinds of spaces allow us to unpack what the patriarchy actually is. Yet, as women we are conditioned to be extremely aware of its presence and the requirements it places on our behavior, thoughts, desires, dreams, appearance, expectations, etc. At the same time, we are conditioned *not* to see it –it is just the way things are; it is normal. Therefore, women and girls are not automatically given tools for recognizing and challenging the patriarchy and its effect on our individual and collective lives.

The patriarchal world culture is bad for everyone, just like sexism, racism, homophobia, transphobia, ageism, xenophobia, and all systems of institutionalized oppression and ideologies of hate and discrimination are bad for everyone. I have found that the more I am aware of how I am affected by these systems and ideologies, the more I can challenge their hold over my life. This is difficult, lifelong work, but I can't think of anything more rewarding or more necessary. Plus, it is totally, 100 percent related to our call to ministry. This is how we do justice, love mercy, and walk humbly with God. (Micah 6:8) This is how we partner with God to bring good news to the poor, to proclaim release to the captives, recovery of sight to the blind, and to let the oppressed go free. (Luke 4:18) None of us are going to do this work perfectly. But perfect is not the point. Being faithful, courageous and willing to risk offending the church for the sake of the church is the point.

Walk the Talk

I reached the point of wanting more and better from the church and my own ministry not long after I began serving in my first call out of seminary. In many ways it was an amazing first job. The congregation was wonderful – progressive, justice-oriented, welcoming, and diverse. And, after about a year, I started to get restless. I was serving in the Cathedral in the heart of the Diocese – you don't get much more "in the center of power" than that. While I genuinely enjoyed much of my work there, dysfunctional patriarchal systems do what they do – they damage.

I won't get into the details or specifics; they don't actually matter. The bottom line is that I struggled to be the kind of leader I wanted to be. My relationships were not what I needed or desired from the people I was doing ministry with. And because I felt we were not "walking the talk" that we preached every Sunday, it was really, really hard to feel we had integrity in our ministries as a whole. I know these are harsh words. It wasn't fun to live through. And what really sucks is that every single woman clergy person that I know has at least one similar story.

We can't change what we don't face. Facing our truth, also known as awareness, is the first part of the process. Telling your truth to someone else and being witnessed in your truth is another part of the process. It turns out I did not have to look far to find colleagues who had similar frustrations, desires, and longings; who were dying to witness and be witnessed as well. The trick was finding people who were not only willing to be honest about it, but who were willing to actually try a different way of being. Not just a different way of *doing* church, a *different way of being church*.

I'm guessing you are not only looking for a different way to be, you are ready to be different. I would imagine you are champing at the bit to create your dream ministry that will reignite your passion and provide you with the context to fully become the bad*ss priest you were born to be.

We Are All We've Got (And All We Need)

Before we go any further, I'm going to let you in on a little secret. There is no new model for doing church. I know everyone is looking for it, but it doesn't exist! At least, there is no *one* new model for doing church. There is no 10-step plan to implement, no fool proof curriculum to download, no program you can share with your parish to double your

ASA (average Sunday attendance) and bring back your joy.

There is something better. There is the freedom to stop worrying about that sh*t (which deep down you know is sh*t). There is the permission to stop worrying about what other people are going to think of you. And there is the gumption already inside of you to just do it already – "it" being the thing you desire and long to do.

Right now, you may believe you don't know what "it" is. I will not make you give up that belief just yet. I do want you to consider that you have *some* idea what it is. Consider the possibility that both things are true – you don't know and you do know. Because some part of you knows. We just have to give her the mic and coax her on stage.

No matter what, you are not alone in this. You are right where you are mean to be. There is a great cloud of sister-priests forming, that God has been slowly bringing together over time, and we have got you. The way forward will be revealed. It is even possible that way can include staying in the church and living a life you love. You just have to be ready to both know and not know. Ready? Great! Let's do this.

CHAPTER 2

The Bridge: Getting from Here to There

———— ◆ ————

"Progress is only possible through longing and as the path of progress is infinite, there should be infinite longing. Thus longing becomes itself a form of the infinite, to be desired for its own sake. This is why the mystics idealize longing. The other name for longing is love."

– IRINA TWEEDIE

Getting Comfortable with Being Uncomfortable

How do you go from desire and longing to creating and doing? Well, again, this is not a twelve-step program (although maybe it should be ...). This is not just "the ultimate guide to being a bad*ss priest and creating a ministry you love." This is *the art of feminine spiritual leadership.* It is an *art.* Truthfully, I am not even going to teach you how to do anything you don't already know how to do. I am going to accompany you on a journey where I will share with you parts of my story and some of the tools and practices I have learned and developed along the way. Then you are going to take them, use them, maybe even tweak them to make your own magic.

The question is, are you ready? Because to get from here to where you want to be you have to cross a bridge. Which means going out to the edge, and then going even further ... into the unknown. At this point I am going to invite you, and even encourage you, to get comfortable with the unknown. Get used to not knowing what is next. Become friends with the "not knowing." Because even when, in the future, you finally figure out what you want to do and how to do it, eventually your old friend not knowing is going to mosey back into town as soon as the next new thing starts to pull at you from the future. So you might as well get well acquainted with her now.

Here is your first tool! We will start with something familiar and easy: a prayer/meditation.

The "I Don't Know Mantra" Tool:

- Find a comfortable seated position.
- Take a few deep breaths, in through your nose and out through your mouth.
- Close your eyes.
- Repeat to yourself this prayer/mantra: "I don't know ..."
- Variations of this prayer might look like:
    ~ "I don't know what I am doing."
    ~ "I don't know what is next."
    ~ "I don't know who I really am."
- Notice what feelings come up. Panic? Anxiety? A tension in your stomach? A pain in your shoulder? Notice what you feel both physically and emotionally. Just notice. And feel it.

- Take a few more deep breaths.
- Repeat to yourself the prayer/mantra: "It is okay. It is all going to be okay. It is okay that I don't know. I am not supposed to know right now. I will know when it is time to know. God knows."
- Repeat until you feel a sense of calm or until ten minutes have passed, whichever comes first.
- Spend some time journaling about the experience.

The "I Don't Know" mantra exercise is all about training yourself to be comfortable with not knowing – also known as being an honest and authentic human being. The patriarchy would have us believe good leaders have all the answers all the time. That is bullsh*t and everyone knows it. Deep down, people want to hear you, as their leader, admit what you don't know when you don't know it so that 1) they can trust you because a) you are telling them the truth and b) you are telling *yourself* the truth and 2) they can see you modeling courage and vulnerability at the same time. This is a superpower. It is also one of the arts of feminine spiritual leadership.

Do We Really Have to Label This "Feminine"?

Now might be a good time to address why I am engaging in the exercise of identifying certain ways of leading as "feminine." The short answer is because traditionally, certain characteristics that actually make for good leadership have been devalued and dismissed because they are associated with the feminine. All people, no matter their gender identification (or non-identification) can benefit from cultivating the leadership qualities I am labeling here as feminine. I do not intend to suggest they need be exclusively or even ultimately labeled as feminine. But for this moment in our human existence, the exercise of naming, claiming, and promoting ways of being that are feminine as extraordinary leadership qualities will help us move us forward out of the patriarchy and into new realm of human dignity and value for all. My end goal is not to replace one half of a duality with its counterpart, but to move us into a flow that takes us beyond where we have ever been before. I am suggesting we use all of the resources at our disposal to be first fully who we are so we can then become the new creations God is calling us to be. Okay, back to our regularly scheduled programming.

Building the Bridge as We Walk It

How do you know if you are ready to cross the bridge? For me, I knew when I felt like I had come to the end of the edge of the church and I still wanted more. I spent ten or so years chipping away at the institutional church structure, trying to create a space for myself where I could claim my role as a leader and build communities of people who both loved the church and desired to change it. I quickly learned "the center" was *not* the place for me. Yes, my whiteness and my upper middle-class status keeps me in the center, but my femaleness and queerness keep me on the margins. And I prefer it that way. Jesus was on the margins. He called people from the margins and to the margins. The only way to destabilize the center is to move everyone to an edge

– then you create a giant circle, rather than a tier with a few on the top and the majority on the bottom. (And circles are very feminine.)

I liked the edge, for a while. I did a lot there and in many ways I was very successful. But after a few years of doing "missional" and "emergent" ministry, trying to keep one foot in the traditional church and one foot on the margins, I looked down and realized I had both feet on the edge– like I was standing on the edge of a cliff. I had a choice. I could lament reaching "the end" and sit down and pout, or I could look out at the horizon. I chose to look out. For a while, I saw nothing but clouds and mist. It was lonely. It was frustrating. And then the clouds began to part and I saw that there was a huge, vast ocean out there. There was so much more beyond the church! I had known this, but I had forgotten. It was time for something more. It was time for something different. It was time for a radical change. It was time for me to let go of the priest I thought I should be and start to become the woman I desired to be – that *God* desired me to be. It was time to step out onto the bridge.

This is where the metaphor gets a bit wonky. Or interesting. Let's say interesting. You know that saying, "we are building the plane as we fly it"? Well, in our case, we are building the bridge as we walk on it. Our job is to keep discerning, keep walking, keep risking, keep going. It is God's job to help with the details and the directions, like a holy GPS. Our job is to desire the trip and the general destination. God will help us get there and figure out exactly where *there* is.

I knew my desire was to help transform the church to be more inclusive, more accepting, more forgiving, more honest, more self-reflective, more compassionate, more just, more in tune with the flow of the Spirit – you know, all the things I want for myself! Easy, right? Piece-of-cake. Turns out, at the core, all this work is *relational* (again, typically feminine). That, my friend, is what makes it so d*mn hard. And it is what makes it so unbelievably amazing.

It Is All About Relationships

All transformational work is relational. Which also means much of the work the church considers *spiritual* is also *relational.* The spiritual life entails constant work on our relationships with ourselves, each other, God and all of creation. This has been my constant refrain since seminary. The art of feminine spiritual leadership is *fundamentally relational.* While you and I learned quite a bit in seminary about humanity's relationship with God and how to invite people and communities deeper into that relationship with God, our instruction for how to nurture and grow inter-personal relationships, or our relationships with ourselves, was minimal. Sure, "self-care" got a fair amount of air time, but a few years of real world ministry make it abundantly clear to anyone with a pulse that, as a group, clergy are not the best at self-care. And while our American culture sells self-improvement, and practically demands it, most of what we are buying doesn't necessarily equate to an uptick in our actual care for ourselves.

As I have teetered along, building my bridge to the other side, many of the tools I have found most useful come from psychology, sociology, even physiology. They are all thoroughly spiritual practices, but they are not things I learned in seminary. I came across each of these practices at varying points in my life when I was searching for different things. Always, the overarching theme was my search for more love and deeper connection – with myself, the people closest to me, my communities, God, and even the cosmos.

I know I'm repeating myself, but this book is not a framework. It is not a guide to follow exactly the way I did it. The patriarchy would have me give you a process; instead, I am going to give you myself and invite you to experience your own restoration. Together we are on a journey. It will have some twists and turns that neither of us see coming. I feel called to share with you what has helped get me to this point. Because other women have shared their stories and their life's work with me, which has helped move me forward. And that's the point, I think – we are in this together.

What to Expect

In Chapter 3, I am going to encourage you to start by finding yourself right, right where you are. Women are really good at loving everyone else, but not so great at loving ourselves. This matters because there are pretty much only two commandments and one of them says, "Love your neighbor as yourself." We will revisit and spend some time on the "as yourself" part.

In Chapter 4, we will look at how having a healthy relationship with yourself is essential for the health of all your relationships and why it is essential for your ministry.

In Chapters 5, 6, and 7 respectively, we will look at your relationships with others, God, and creation. These relationships are not only interrelated but their health and wholeness is bound up with one another. Practicing the art of feminine spiritual leadership involves attending to each of these relationships individually and collectively, honoring the fundamental relationality of leadership and ministry.

In Chapter 8, we go deep with one of our ultimate superpowers – our feelings! I know, I can tell you are excited. We will start by exploring how to pay particular attention to our feelings as valuable means of receiving information and as a way we communicate with the divine. We will also learn an excellent dialogue tool for communicating more effectively with others that encourages both parties to feel seen, valued, and heard.

In Chapter 9, we will reintroduce ourselves to the notion that our bodies are not only repositories of wisdom but communicators of wisdom as well! In this chapter we will learn skills and practices for unlearning our disdain for our female bodies, connecting to the divinity within our bodies, and using our bodies as power vehicles and containers for our leadership.

In Chapter 10, you will be invited to take perhaps the greatest leap of trust and faith of our journey together and stretch yourself to consider the power of pleasure. We will learn in this chapter how connecting to our desires is a way of directly connecting to our divine calling, and following our pleasure is a key to following God's movement in our lives. This concept will be difficult to embrace at first, because it goes against everything the patriarchal church has taught us and taught us to teach others! I'm going to ask you to trust me on this one. We will take our time getting there, and by Chapter 10 I hope and pray you are ready for the life-altering invitation to the spiritual pursuit of pleasure.

In the final chapter, we will end with one of the most important elements involved in practicing the art of feminine spiritual leadership – the realization that we are not meant to do ministry alone. Not only are we not meant to do ministry alone, engaging in ministry with our sisters is the only way to step fully into our own leadership. As we come to the end of this book's journey together, our continued journey together as sister priests in ministry begins.

Now, it is time to step out into the unknown and trust your foot will hit the bridge. Ready? One ... two ... three ... go!

CHAPTER 3

Right Where You Are

———— ◆ ————

*"To be yourself in a world that is constantly trying
to make you something else is the
greatest accomplishment."*
– Ralph Waldo Emerson

Self-Hate – Who, Me?

A few years ago, I realized something incredibly sad – I
could not remember a time when I was completely happy
with myself. I had this realization during a particularly difficult stretch of time when I was struggling with my body
image and my weight in particular. At thirty years old I had
managed to do some pretty significant things with my life –
I had graduated college, received two masters degrees from
Yale, been ordained, traveled extensively, cultivated good
relationships with friends, and found an amazing person to
love. By most measures of "success," I was doing well.

I remember one day I was feeling particularly good – I
had just had a fun lunch with a friend, and the weather
outside was gorgeous so I was walking home through my
neighborhood, stopping in and out of shops and riding a
wave of joy and satisfaction. And then I saw my reflection
in a store window. My immediate thought was, "Ugh, I
look so fat." My joy evaporated, my spirit plummeted, and
all my self-worth went right out that store window.

F*ck. It wasn't just that the reflection I saw in the window looked fatter than I felt. It wasn't just that a familiar trigger sent a self-criticism signal down a well-worn pathway in my brain. It was that this automatic response I had learned over time *stole my joy*. It changed my reality. If I had not seen my reflection and had that opportunity to fall into self-hate mode, I would have continued sauntering down the sidewalk until I reached my house and gone on with my day feeling pretty good. Of course, how long would that have lasted? Until some opportunity came up where I could fall back into self-hate. Because ultimately, that was my default pattern.

I started to notice all the ways I automatically said hateful things to myself. I began to force myself to pay attention to my self-critical thoughts. Every woman alive is a professional self-criticizer. It is what we are trained to do. Other authors have focused extensively on the ways the patriarchal world culture has trained women to hate ourselves, and I will offer some suggestions for further reading at the end of this book because I firmly believe we all need to get very clear about the enemy we are up against – and the enemy is the patriarchal world culture.

I never thought I would be a feminist crusader and that is not a label I claim for myself. But the more I pay attention to the messages the outside world is feeding me, the more I become aware of how indoctrinated I have become by those messages telling me some version of "I am not good enough or worthy enough," and the more I am convinced that in order to break this cycle and release myself from the hold these beliefs have over me I must be able to recognize them for what they are and reject them in order to live any other way.

Brainwashed by the PWC (Patriarchal World Culture)

I know I am making this sound like a really big deal, because I think it is. Have you ever thought it was perfectly natural that you are your harshest critic? Have you ever caught yourself *feeling bad about feeling good about yourself*, particularly your appearance or your abilities or your intellect? Women are walking around in knots, believing this is somehow both all in our heads and all our fault. We all need help to realize 1) it is not our fault and 2) it doesn't have to be this way.

You may be wondering why I am starting a book about creating your dream ministry with a tangent about self-hate and self-love. There are a few reasons. First, if you are able to create your dream ministry but do not do the work of overcoming your underlying feelings of self-hate, you will never love your life, because you will not really love yourself. Second, you will not be ready for your dream ministry until you become the person who is capable of receiving it. Lastly, you have to become the woman who is ready to receive her dream ministry first, before you will be able to create it.

This last one is the most difficult to understand, because it is not a head trip, it is a mind/body/soul trip. If you could intellectually scheme your way to your dream ministry and perfect life, you would have done it already. This book is less about thinking (you know how to do that) and more about feeling, being, and receiving – a.k.a. the stuff you need to work on.

You don't have to understand it now. Just come along for the ride. If you read this book and you try using some of the tools, practices, rituals, and magic spells I will teach you to unearth your superpowers but at the end you are like, "Thanks, Sara, this isn't for me," I will not be upset and I will bless you as you continue on your way.

But, if you try some of the things I suggest and you start to notice a shift, I will encourage you with every cell in my body to keep going! Because the more we practice these ways of being, the more we become the bad*ss priests we were born to be. The church and the world desperately need us to be those priests. And, even more so, we need ourselves to be those women.

Finding Yourself Right

Time for another tool! This tool comes in handy when you find yourself in a situation like I did, staring at my reflection in the store window and the automatic thought pops into your head, piercing your own heart, "Ugh, you are so fat."

The thought might look like something else for you. It can take a bazillion forms a day. Common forms are:

- "That was really stupid."
- "Wow, you really f*cked that up."
- "They don't really like you."
- "I hate my (insert body part)."
- "Why did I just do that?"

- "What is wrong with me?"
- "Why am I still struggling with this?"
- "I am never going to (insert thing you desire to do or be)."

These are just a few examples. Go ahead, write out your own. Just think over the last 24 hours and you will be able to come up with your own list of five to ten. Then look at your list – these thoughts are indicators that you are in a state I refer to as "In Disapproval of Yourself"

In Disapproval of Yourself

Being "In Disapproval of Yourself" is like being in a place you know is bad for you but is just so d*mn comfortable that you never want to leave. You know every nook and cranny of "In Disapproval of Yourself." It feels like home; an abusive home, but home nonetheless.

Well, my dear, it's time to leave home. Here is how you do it:

1. Recognize you are In Disapproval of Yourself (IDOY).

2. Thank yourself for creating this home for yourself! (Because really, disapproval of yourself has been a coping mechanism for surviving the PWC. And so far, it has worked. You are still alive, aren't you? However, now it is time to go a step up from surviving.

3. Choose to leave "Disapproval" by "Finding Yourself Right."

The "Finding Yourself Right" Tool:

Finding Yourself Right involves the following process:

1. Stop what you are doing! Do not beat yourself up any more about whatever thought you had or thing you did that put you IDOY.

2. Recognize and affirm yourself as the genius you are. Because no matter what you are doing or what you are thinking or what is happening, you are always a genius. You are a woman, you are a genius – it is just a given. Accept this truth now.

3. Choose to approve of yourself right where you are. No matter what is going on outside of you or inside of you, nothing can take away your rightness because nothing can take away your worth. Why? Because you are the dwelling place of God. You are the Beloved of the Universe. You are a magnificent creation made in the image of the Divine. This is your evidence that you are right, right where you are. This is your proof. It is time to believe it; like, believe it believe it. You are done living like this is not true. You are done preaching this to everyone else and believing it about everyone else but still treating yourself like a piece of sh*t. No more. That stops right now.

4. Repeat steps 1–3 every time you catch yourself IDOY. Un-learning takes time. Creating new neural pathways takes time. Repeat, repeat, repeat.

Awesome! You are doing so well. This may either seem like a really small thing to try to do or a really big thing.

Either way, you are correct. These tools will allow you to make small adjustments in your thinking that over time will add up to a huge shift in awareness, which over more time will help you unlearn your self-hate practices and relearn deep and true love for yourself.

Let's practice right now. One way to practice identifying places you may be IDOY is to take stock of what you are struggling with. I'm going to suggest some common struggles women have and you see if they resonate.

- You don't know how to stand for your vision when no one else can see it.
- You worry about standing up to people in power and pissing them off.
- You worry people won't like you.
- You worry about what people will think of you.
- You worry about abusing your power.
- You have seen so many clergy use power poorly, you are not sure how to do it well.
- You look around the church and you see few if any models of being a female priest that feel familiar or look like anything you want to aspire to.
- You have been told, and therefore you worry, that you are too opinionated.
- You have been told, and therefore you worry, that you are too academic.
- You have been told, and therefore you worry, that you are too passionate.
- You have been told, and therefore you worry, that you are too emotional.

- You have been told, and therefore you worry, that you are too progressive.
- You have been told, and therefore you worry, that you are too trusting.
- You have been told, and therefore you worry, that you are too earnest.
- You have been told, and therefore you worry, you expect too much of others.
- Rarely, if ever, are you told you are (fill in the blank) enough.
- Rarely, if ever, do you *feel* you are (fill in the blank) enough.

Ugh, that was pretty awful, wasn't it? See what disapproval of yourself feels like!

After all that, you know what is really crazy? You can feel all those things and at the same time another part of you knows you have a unique and powerful voice, knows you are an excellent preacher, knows people trust and look up to you, knows you have an amazing power to love and care for people even when they drive you crazy, knows you are a good priest and you could be a kick-*ss priest, if only all these different parts of yourself would just get on the same page!

No wonder you feel stuck! All of these things feel like impossible contradictions and yet you still manage to either (1) feel them all at once or (2) oscillate back and forth between them at lightning speed. As a woman, you can shapeshift, or rather "emotion-shift," with the best of them. The problem is not that we have been taught to believe two opposing things about ourselves at the same time (i.e., that we are too much and yet not enough). Being two different things at once is easy. *Only two different things?* Ha! We are women; we are walking dichotomies in heels. The problem is we have been trained to believe things about ourselves that are just not true.

It is not a coincidence that we feel stuck. There are many people who have a vested interest in you and I staying stuck as well as in our believing that we need to figure out what and how we need to change before we start to lead in the ways we feel called. The longer we believe we are "stuck," the longer we wait for permission and outside validation, and the longer others stay in power.

Here is the thing – there is absolutely nothing wrong with you.

Take a minute to let that sink in.

There is absolutely nothing wrong with you.

Forming a list of all the reasons why that is not true? There is more evidence of your training. Now that we are learning the art of feminine spiritual leadership we must always be on the lookout for evidence of our patriarchal training, so we can practice unlearning what the PWC wants us to believe about who we are, and we can practice re-learning what God would have us believe about who we are.

The PWC trains us to believe we are not good enough, not smart enough, not pretty enough, not talented enough, not spiritual enough, not together enough ... the list goes on indefinitely. And, *at the very same time,* we have been trained to believe we are too much! Too opinionated ... aw, screw it, I'm not making another list. It is enough to make all the women in the world crazy and then tell us to stop being hysterical. Bottom line, we have been intentionally taught to disapprove of ourselves.

I Once Was Blind but Now I See

How many times have you done your best to please everyone and end up pleasing no one? Let me rephrase that. How many *years* have you spent trying to please everyone but ended up pleasing no one? Eventually we learn that trying to please everyone never works, but that mandate is so deeply engrained in us it can take even more years to finally allow yourself not to try anymore. Then the question becomes, who do you please? Your boss (assuming you have one), your congregation (which is hardly a unanimous entity), God (hardly an exact science).

And what about what *you* want? Yes, it is finally time to go there. When was the last time you thought about what you want? When was the last time you allowed yourself to make a decision based on what you want? When was the last time you allowed yourself to make a decision based on what you want *regardless of what other people thought or felt about it?*

I was never more preoccupied by what others wanted of me and for me than when I was in the ordination process. When I was discerning whether to be ordained I spent so much time trying to figure out what I was *supposed* to do. I had hoped what I was supposed to do would be made clear through contemplating a mash-up of Frederick Buechner and Howard Thurman quotes. I was supposed to do what made me come alive and what met the world's deepest needs. I knew my calling was to be found somewhere in there. But to get there I had to hack through the weeds of what everyone else said I was supposed to do, which more often than not was some version of putting God first by serving others and putting myself last. The way of self-denial. No one else seemed to notice how dangerous this was to tell a woman....

The patriarchal church tells us our vocations are not about what we want but about what God wants, as if they are mutually exclusive. We are told over and over again we cannot do anything on our own without God, we are not good enough without God, we are not worthy of this calling ... without God. I'm sorry, but I thought our baptism and the gift of the Holy Spirit meant we are never without God and that God, in fact, dwells inside of us?

Seems like the emphasis here is that we better not trust ourselves, and boy have we taken that to heart. Good thing we can trust the church to tell us what God wants. (I'm hoping you know me well enough by now to know when I'm kidding ... I'm kidding.) Let's just stop for a moment and ask how well this is working out for everyone involved. I'm thinking it is not working so well.

What happened to serving from the place where our deepest joy and the world's deepest needs meet? Not where they wave at each other from across the room or reminisce about how they were once ships passing in the night, but where they *meet.* Do you even know where that meeting place is anymore?

Believing You Are Enough

Fundamentally, on a soul level, on a body/mind/spirit level, on an essence of our humanity level, on a being level, *there is nothing wrong with us.* We are fundamentally *right.* (Remember, we learned this earlier in this chapter!) We are fundamentally *good.* I'm pretty sure it says that in scripture somewhere (see Genesis). Even if you want to go with the notion of "the fall" and talk about how there are parts of us as human beings that are broken and separated from God, denying those parts is not how they are redeemed.

God redeems what is sinful in us and makes us whole. Sin is not something we *are.* No human being is so infected with sin that they are irredeemable, right? Our darkest parts, our biggest mistakes, our greatest failings – none of those things can change our fundamental "is-ness" which is good, which is of God, which is Imago Dei, which is divine. *Nothing undoes that.* Nothing undoes grace. Nothing undoes goodness. Even when we are in the midst of the biggest pile of sh*t (i.e., sin, evil, whatever) we are never cut off from our source, our power, our truth, our connection to God.

So, what does all this mean? This means that no matter where we are, no matter what is going on with us or in us, no matter how much we have been trained and enculturated to believe that we are wrong and bad, we must, must, must make a different choice and choose instead to find ourselves right and to believe we are enough.

This shift in thinking is of the smallest degree and yet it is incredibly, incredibly hard. It is the choice between disapproving of yourself or approving of yourself right where you are. It is the choice between believing the lies the patriarchal world culture tells you or believing what God tells you. It is the choice between trusting the world or trusting yourself.

Here is a tool for practicing believing you are enough. It is called "The Enoughness Affirmation."

The "Enoughness Affirmation" Tool:

- Take a deep breath in through your nose and let it out through your mouth. Repeat this two more times.
- The next time you breathe in through your nose say to yourself, either silently or aloud, "Just as I am, I am enough."
- Continue to breathe in and out slowly, repeating the phrase to yourself.
- Continue repeating the phrase until something shifts and you feel ready to stop.
- Say the affirmation any time you question your enoughness.

Reframe, Reframe, Reframe

Believing you are enough is 100 percent an inside job. When you notice yourself beating up on yourself, hit the pause button – have compassion for yourself. You are only doing what you have been taught to do, which is talk to yourself like your own worst enemy. We would never talk to a friend the way we talk to ourselves. Hell, we would never talk to an enemy the way we talk to ourselves! We treat ourselves much worse than we would ever dare treat another person. Awareness of and compassion for our own inner dialogue is a huge step toward shifting into a way of self-love.

After awareness and compassion comes introducing the new idea. What if, instead, you choose to tell yourself *you are enough and more than enough*? This is the beginning of reframing your experience and changing how you engage with your experience. Allow yourself to consider, "If I am enough ... what else might be true?"

Finding Yourself Right is an example of reframing. Remember how I said you were a genius? In everything that you do, the choices you make or don't make, the conscious and unconscious way you structure your life, God is always working things out for the good of those who love God (Romans 8:28). When you reframe, you can begin to practice believing that everything you have done and everything that has happened to you up until that moment is *exactly right*. Once you have made that cognitive reframe you can practice telling yourself an entirely different story about who you are and how you got here.

All of these tools are to be used to help you take what you believe theologically and infuse those beliefs into what you think about yourself so you can practice loving yourself the way God loves you. The tools give our theology direct access to our self-talk. We *believe* God works all things for the good of those who love God. We *believe* we are made in the image of God. We *believe* God's Holy Spirit dwells with us. Well, if we believe all these things, wouldn't it be good to start talking to ourselves as if they were true?

The word "believe" in old English can also be translated as "be love." What we believe has the power to create our realities. If those beliefs are not creating a reality where we can "be love" then what are they creating? And do we want to continue to believe them?

I Think Therefore I Am

We have the power to create and un-create worlds with our thoughts. It is scary to admit we have this power, but whether we admit it or not we do it all the time! When we change our self-talk, we change our internal world and when we change our internal world we are much more capable of changing our external world.

There is a huge market for "self-help" and "personal development." These are not innately bad things; in fact, our relationship with ourselves is of central importance to a life well-lived, including our ability to minister to others. However, the crux of many of these self-help agendas is that there is something outside of yourself that you *need* (to learn, to become, to master) that you can only access through someone else. The patriarchal paradigm says some teach and others learn, some are masters and some are slaves, some are the keepers and some are the seekers. This is another example of where our limited understanding and duality trip us up. We are all always *both*.

There is something about claiming the authority of the both/and that gives many women pause. It means basically saying we reject the dominant ways the world categorizes, well, everyone, and says we hold ourselves outside of or above these paradigms. And who are we to do that? Who are we to reject centuries of understanding and methodologies and ways of being and say we have something better? A bad*ss priest, that's who!

The courage that lies deep within us is intimidating. It is supposed to be. We are right to be a bit apprehensive, a bit cautious, a bit scared. The power we are about to unleash is going to create some major changes, and we should not come at these changes lightly. We are also learning to recognize that this power within us comes from a power greater than us. The reason we are able to express such courage and wisdom and drive is because we are a part of a force at work that is greater than ourselves. We access this power not through self-denial but through self-awareness, particularly our awareness of our desires and longings. We will talk more about this in the next chapter.

In our journeys toward leading as ourselves, we must reclaim and reimagine many things we have been taught to hate or avoid or dismiss or discount, particularly those parts of ourselves that are dark, or that the patriarchy says are weakness. This is the heart of the work of feminine spiritual leadership. Those denied parts of ourselves are very often our superpowers and we are going to need every one of our superpowers to create a life and ministry we love – not to mention to help to heal the patriarchal church!

Our Worth Is Non-Negotiable

I believed, for a long time, that I had to follow the rules and do what other people wanted me to do in order for them to love me. This included how I approached my ministry and my priesthood. My value and my worth lay in my obedience and my ability to perform and produce based on another person's measurements and desires. I still struggle with this. It is not a fun way to live.

Untangling myself from learned disapproval will be a lifelong journey. Every day I must choose to practice a new way of being where I not only believe my value comes from inside myself rather than outside of myself, but I treat myself and talk to myself as if that were true. Finding myself right, believing I am enough, and reframing my experiences from a place of self-love are not meant to be tools to help me become a better person and priest so that I can create a ministry I love. I'm going to let the cat out of the bag early – the reason to use these tools is not simply to create a ministry you love or be a bad*ss priest. The real work is becoming the woman, the person, you are meant to be. And a fundamental element of this is liking and loving yourself, which is the focus of the next chapter. Yes, this work will have amazing effects on your ministry, but I'm more interested in the effects it has on you and your life. No matter what your ASA is, I want you to know this in your bones and speak these words to yourself– *my worth is non-negotiable.* Your goodness and lovability are not up for debate.

As I have begun to practice loving myself in this way, all my relationships have had to change – not just my relationship with myself but my relationships with my family, my spouse, my community, other women, other cultures, the world, the cosmos, God, all of it. I have had to go from being a relentless seeker of evidence that I am not good enough to a fierce proclaimer of my worth. In real life this looks like speaking up when I feel I have been mistreated by a colleague, rather than swallowing my feelings and "moving on." It looks like pausing my negative self-talk when I become aware of myself saying to myself, "You said you were going to write two chapters today and you didn't even finish one. You suck...."It looks like reframing this thought from the foundation that I am enough and compassionately saying to myself instead, "You did the best you could today. What you wrote was excellent. You are good. You are enough."

I know it sounds super cheesy, but you know what, I know it is working. Because I notice myself having less automatic self-hating thoughts and more automatic compassionate thoughts. Yay neuroplasticity! And yay FSL (Feminine Spiritual Leadership) tools! Ready for more?

CHAPTER 4

Your Relationship with Your Self

———◆———

"True belonging is the spiritual practice of believing in and belonging to yourself so deeply that you can share your most authentic self with the world and find sacredness in both being a part of something and standing alone in the wilderness. True belonging doesn't require you to change who you are; it requires you to be who you are."

– BRENÉ BROWN, BRAVING THE WILDERNESS

Who Do You Want to Be?

Before I was ordained but while I was still in the ordination process, I had a conversation with a clergy person in a position of power over me about the kind of ministry I felt I was called to. Tentatively, I shared I did not feel I would spend my entire career in traditional parish ministry. For the next few minutes we tossed back and forth standard "alternative" ministry settings I could consider – chaplaincy, teaching, church planting, etc. – all of which I said I was open to. Then I commented that I was still discerning what kind of priest I wanted to be. His response was to tell me not to focus on what I wanted to be but to focus on what I "wanted to do."

I sat with this advice for a long time and even tried to apply it. I found the problems with this approach to be twofold. First, when I allowed myself to think about what I wanted to do, the options were innumerable. There were so many options for ministries that I could do that would be fine, even great, it was completely overwhelming. The second thing I noticed is harder to name. It has to do with authenticity and integrity. Discernment is a lifelong endeavor—in every moment we are discerning how we want to show up. When you are grounded in an understanding of who you desire to be and who God has created and called you to be, then what you do will flow from that place.

This also has to do with how we understand our identity and where we find our worth. If we make what we do what defines us (which is what most of the world does, thanks patriarchy) several things happen. Our worth is tied to our success and our productivity- two things that are in constant flux and in many ways not in our ultimate control. Secondly, what happens when we cannot or choose not to do the same things anymore? Our entire identity unravels. Lastly, there can develop a disconnect between who we say we are (and believe we are) and what we do. This is where a lot of people have a lot of trouble with Christians. Gandhi noticed it when he said, "I like your Christ, I do not like your Christians. Your Christians are so unlike your Christ."

Yes, Jesus set a high bar for us to meet. Some might argue it is an impossible bar. The only way we can get remotely close to "perfect as God in heaven is perfect" is with grace and forgiveness. So, we better rely heavily on grace and forgiveness then. And while, yes, we should endeavor to enact grace and perform acts of forgiveness, those are two examples of defining Christian characteristics that we cannot do anything to warrant or earn. We receive grace. We are forgiven. That is who we are and who we are called to become. Grounding ourselves in that identity and allowing God's Spirit to work through us is what enables us to do anything, let alone ministry.

When I focused on what I want *to do* I have felt something disconnect inside of me, like a plug being pulled from its socket. It was not until much later that I could identify this "unplugged" feeling as a disconnection from both God and my own desires. It is a relational disconnect. This is at the heart of why Christians an spend so much time "doing" church" but not nearly as much time "being" church. This problem is, at its heart, relational; it is about who we are.

In the last few years, my denomination (the Episcopal Church) has been preoccupied with discerning how we can change our institutional structures to better serve our mission. Personally, I don't think any changes the institutional church could make to our programming, structure, liturgy, or polity will do anything substantial to ultimately stop the hemorrhaging of members or the inevitable death of our current form, because those things are not the core problem. Our problem is *relational.*

It Is Not (Only) What We Do,
It Is Who We Are

There is a reason Jesus cut through the crap and told us there are fundamentally only two commandments – love God and love our neighbor as ourselves. Currently our church does not have a functional or healthy theology of self-love, let alone healthy self-love practices. In fact, we have the opposite. We have a theology of self-denial bordering on self-annihilation. Why? Because of intentional biblical interpretation of select biblical verses. If there is one thing I learned in seminary it is that you can make the bible say anything you want and find theological backing for nearly any argument.

"If any want to become my followers, let them deny themselves and take up their cross and follow me." A version of this verse is found in all three synoptic gospels. Like many verses in the Bible, it has been used to subdue, rebuke, and control those who would stand up for their own rights and the rights of others. While the case can be made that there are instances in which denying the version of "yourself" that stands in opposition to God and God's will is the way to follow Christ, self-denial as a blanket practice is an incredibly dangerous maxim to demand. This is especially true when the demand is being made by those with power who laud self-denial over those who are already oppressed and marginalized as the only way they can truly and faithfully serve God.

Yes, we must love God and love our neighbor as ourselves. However, if we do not know how to love ourselves, how can we be expected to love our neighbors well? As a church, the story we tell ourselves is that we are in the business of loving God and loving neighbor and we are the best at what we do. A brief consideration of the "customer feedback" we are receiving—i.e. people voting with their feet, right out the door—would indicate we might want to reexamine just how well we are doing.

The problem is our actual problem is a lot more difficult and painful to face than the problems we like to believe we have. It is a lot easier to try and figure out how to do worship differently, or change how we structure ourselves, or think of new ways of doing evangelism, than it is to admit how we fundamentally relate to one another needs a lot of work. Just like anything else, the only way through this is to go through this. And there is an enormous amount of resistance to even acknowledging our relational problems let alone a commitment to doing the work to address problems. But this is the work; the gospel work. And, like most things, it starts with us.

Let It Go

If we are going to lead the church in being something new, then we must start with ourselves. The good news is, just like we are exactly where we are meant to be, and the church is exactly where she needs to be. I truly believe this. The church as we know it is changing and dying because that is exactly what needs to happen.

As Christians, this is our story—we should know how this works! And yet, because we are human, we resist the fact that this is how transformation works. I don't know about you, but I keep thinking I will get to the point in my life as a Christian and as a priest where I will finally "get it" and I won't need to die anymore. No such luck. The good news is we don't have to convince each other that death and resurrection is the way God works; we have bought into that story. The bad news is we still have a lot of work to do getting our theological beliefs to infiltrate the rest of our selves.

Try as we might, there is no way to hack resurrection to avoid death. Again, awareness is the first step. Let's go ahead and stop trying. When we reframe this situation we find ourselves in, we can see that we are actually being given an amazing opportunity to practice being the people God is calling us to be and to modeling the type of leadership we desire.

I'm going to warn you: this next tool is going to be a little weird. I mentioned already that for me this process of becoming the woman and the priest God created me to be has included letting go of the leader I *thought* I had to be to please the church. One day, as I was pondering how I could both stay in the church and minister with integrity, I felt the need to literally bury my old-priest-self. So much had happened that I was no longer her. She was dead and I needed to do more than singing Taylor Swift songs, I needed to perform a liturgy. So that is exactly what I did. And I am going to invite you to do the same.

In order to be leaders who take people through the journey of death and resurrection we have to know the terrain so well we can walk it in the dark. So how are we going to model the death and resurrection cycle for our church? We are going to allow the priest we have been to die. And we are going to give her a proper send off.

Let go of the ministry you have built. Even let go of the dreams you have for the future. Right now, in this moment, let it all go (queue *Frozen* theme song). But seriously, the grasping and striving and resisting who we really are and what is actually going on is making us nuts! The priest you are called to be is a truth teller. The priest who keeps her mouth shut and ignores her instincts has had her day. Your relationship with yourself is changing and it is time to celebrate that.

As a priest you know that when relationships change, which they always do, it is important to mark those changes as well as give ourselves time and space to grieve what has been as we await what will be. Now is your chance to let go of everything that is holding you back in your ministry and offer it up to God.

A "Rite of Burial for Your Former Self" Tool:

You are going to bury your former-priest self. You can do this however you want; feel free to make this ritual your own. Here are a few suggestions.

- Make a list of all the things you thought you had to be to be a good priest. In particular think about the ways you measured success, the ways you sought and received validation from others, the rules (perceived or real) you had to follow, the ways you had to present yourself, the theology you were not so sure about but that is affirmed by your denomination, the ways you had to defer to authority that made you uncomfortable. This is just a place to start. Let it all out.

- Find a picture or an object you feel represents your ministry/priesthood up until this point.
- Set aside some time (20 minutes or so) and go to a place you consider holy that is private enough to perform this ritual.
- Reverently and respectfully dig a hole in the earth and bury your picture/object and your list.
- Conduct a service for your former-priest-self. Give her due to her. Use whatever prayers or liturgy feels right.
- After performing this ritual, take time to journal. Write about what it felt like to let go of this former version of yourself, what you said to honor her and how you are going to commit to being present with yourself as you allow yourself to grieve.

I found myself mourning what I had hoped ministry would be like. When my naïve self died, I mourned for her. And I knew if I was going to go forward and stay in the church *I* needed to change. I had spent years focusing on how I wished the church would change. Just like when we focus on wishing another person would change, eventually we realize that the only person we have control over is ourselves. It starts with us.

Women experience many deaths of our selves throughout our lives. You probably have experienced at least one or two already. Now that you have experienced the death of the priest you were, you have created space for the new bad*ss priest you desire to be. It is time for her to rise.

A Clean Slate

A few years ago, I was a co-founder of an alternative Christian community and in an effort to describe the purpose of our community, our tag line was "Christianity without the crap." It was a noble endeavor. We chose to name ourselves "The Slate Project" because, in effect, the primary question we were asking ourselves was what if we had a clean slate for being the church?

Consider this question for yourself: what kind of priest would you be if you had a clean slate? Because the truth is, you do. One of the biggest perks of being a Christian is that each day, each moment really, we get a clean slate. Our identity, grounded in our relationship with God, is a beloved child of the one Creator, who is constantly being redeemed constantly the recipient of grace. Our main task in response to this reality is to allow this belief in who we are to shape our reality.

Many of the tools and practices we have learned thus far can greatly aid you in your journey toward "cleaning" your relationship "slate" with yourself in order to create a relationship that is more loving. I am going to throw bit of a wrench in the mix now by suggesting that when we work on one relationship, say our relationship with ourselves, it is never fully separate from any of our other relationships, i.e., with others, with God, or with all of creation. When we say we are "focusing on our relationship with ourselves" it is a bit of a mind game we allow ourselves to play when it is helpful, to let ourselves think our relationship with our self is a *thing* that is or can be separate from any of our other relationships; because really, it can't be. But I won't go too far down this philosophical rabbit hole. Suffice it to say, interconnection and interrelatedness are always the reality and our brains can only handle so much at once.

The central ingredient to leading and loving as our true selves is to place attending to and nurturing our relationship with ourselves in its rightful place of importance. This may be the key element involved in the art of feminine spiritual leadership. In that spirit, I am now going to give you permission to do the one thing you may have suspected all along was the one thing you needed to do to turn your ministry around, but rationally, culturally, and ecclesiologically you have been told to avoid at all costs: put yourself first.

Now, I can just imagine a list of all the ways this idea has been abused and misused forming in your mind. I am not suggesting you adopt a form of narcissism, nor am I talking about putting yourself above others and squashing their useless bodies in your wake. I am talking about creating, over time and with practice, automatic receptors within your very self of a never-ending source of love which you intentionally allow to flow through your self *first* so everything you touch and everyone you serve is awash in its overflow. Sound good?

Feminine spiritual leadership, a.k.a leading as our selves, is about leading from a place of pleasure, of deep desire and deep abundance. Abundance is another word that gets misused and over-used in our culture, especially by some evangelical Christians. Here I do not mean abundance in the context of scarcity, where because you have others do not have. I mean abundance from a place of enoughness and more than enoughness.

You would not be shocked to learn that when we are spiritually nourished and fulfilled we are much better leaders. Imagine if seeking your own joy, pleasure, and inspiration was your most important job and, bonus, it actually helped you to better do your job? This does not have to stay a dream... there are things you can do to make it come true.

All Desires Known

I have already shown my hand and told you that I think having a healthy and loving relationship with yourself is fundamental and non-negotiable to being able to have a ministry and a life you love. Now it is time to go even further and challenge yourself to consider that your passion for ministry comes directly from the longings of your heart and the way to access that passion is by getting in touch with your desires.

At one point I thought I was going to call this book *All Desires Known*, as a bit of a secret shout out to my Episcopal sisters who, I hoped, would made the connection with the collect for purity: "Almighty God, to you all hearts are open, *all desires known,* and from whom no secrets are hid." If you are an Episcopal priest, you likely pray this prayer at least once a week. I love the idea that God knows all our desires and this is a holy and righteous thing. Part of the work of claiming our power and passion for ministry is reclaiming our desires. God places God's longings in our hearts. Rather than dismissing or diminishing our desires, we could be exploring them and discerning how those things we especially love and are gifted at are in fact the same things God for us and for our ministry. Are all desires from God? No, just like not all thoughts or feelings or beliefs are from God. But they are just as worth of consideration and discernment as possible clues revealing who we are and who God is calling us to be. This prayer can remind us to commit to ourselves and to God our intention to know and honor our desires as much as God does.

Next on our list of the feminine spiritual leadership arts is lovingly tackling our relationships with God. If the health of our relationships is directly connected to our ability to be bad*ss priests, not to mention to our overall sense of health and well-being, this definitely includes our relationships with God. I realize broaching this topic may feel like opening a can of worms. Or perhaps, this feels like the one relationship you have well in hand. Either way, take some deep breaths, say the enoughness mantra a few times, and meet me in Chapter 5.

Your Relationship with God

———◆———

"You can never trust God too much. Why is it that some people do not bear fruit? It is because they have no trust either in God or in themselves."

– MEISTER ECKHART

God Is Like ...

I was ten years old and I was super frustrated. My family and I had gone to church that morning and I had come home all incensed. The priest had spent much of the sermon telling us about God's will and what God wants for our lives. How could some guy possibly be able to tell us what God's will was? It seemed like an obviously outrageous claim to me and I did not understand why no one else was up in arms.

I sat on the edge of my parents' bed and tried to explain my indignation to my mother. She sat and listened thoughtfully for a while. Then she said, "God is like this" and she made a motion with her hands, waving them back and forth over each other as if she was doing some kind of spiritual rap move. The gesture was meant to show that God is what is in between what we can see or know for sure. How do you have a relationship with something you can never know for sure? Years later I see how that same question could be applied to any relationship, for we can never know another being for sure. But at least in our relationships with other people we can see them, touch them, hear them—communicating with God is a bit different.

Presumably, it would be a given that as a priest you have a relationship with God. But presuming is not much better than assuming, and we all know how well that usually works out. Rather than presume I am going to ask you – how do you know you have a relationship with God? This is not a trick question, but it may be one you have not thought about before. Sure, you have told your spiritual autobiography more times than you can count and at some point, it became the solidified version of the story you always tell when people ask you, "Why did you decide to become a priest?" But this time I want you to think beyond the bounds of your spiritual calling and even your everyday interactions with God and feel into how it is you *experience* God.

Knowing God

How do you experience your relationship with God? Do you sense an emotion stirring inside of you? Do you feel something in your body? Is your experience the same every time? Is it different every time? Have you had one crazy experience of the Divine that was unlike anything you had ever experienced before or since? This is all important information about your unique relationship with God. And your relationship with God is allowed to be unique, it is supposed to be unique.

At least for me, going through the discernment process for ordination often felt like an exercise in taking my experiences of God and squeezing them into a box that church committees could understand and therefore approve of. There were missed opportunities after missed opportunities to explore all the different ways that God was communicating with me. If an experience didn't look like a clear communication from God was calling me to perform the sacraments and to be "set apart" through ordination, then the vibe I got was I probably shouldn't mention it in my "spiritual autobiography."

I have always been fascinated by the myriad of ways we human beings experience and encounter the Divine. I am often surprised and elated when I meet someone who runs in institutional church circles who openly talks about their spiritual life in non-traditional Christian terms. Just the other day at the parish where I am supplying I heard someone on the altar guild say, "The Universe is always communicating with me in the most perfect way!" Hearing this made me so happy. Our traditional Christian ways of talking about God and describing our relationships with God continue to have their place and serve important functions. And, one of the blessings of living during the twenty-first century is the sheer volume of diverse ways of being human and spiritual we are blessed to have access to. We have so much to learn from each other!

God Is Bigger Than the Church

When you work for the institutional church it can be easy to forget that God is bigger than the particular, and limited, ways our denominations, even our religion, understand God. Does it feel a little blasphemous for me to even say this? I know, I get it. Because many of our churches are struggling to define ourselves in a post-Christian climate, we tend to focus on what makes us different from everyone else. It can feel like we are doubling down on our identity— we are who we are because we are not like you! And, by the way, we are right. Doesn't make for stellar ecumenical and interfaith relationships, not to mention how we come across to the folks who are spiritual but not religious.

For as long as human beings have been conscious of our own existence, we have pondered the big, existential questions like, "Why are we here? Where did we come from? Where are we going?" In terms of the many traditional ways of relating to God, it is important to remember that Christian traditions were originally based on Jewish traditions, which were based on polytheistic Canaanite traditions, which were based on pagan and occult traditions. We act like "cafeteria" religion is a new (and bad) thing, but whenever and wherever people from different cultures interact there has always been intermixing and mingling of religious practices. Always. And there have always been (at least) two ways to respond in these situations – share and learn or deny and defend. There is the "my God's way or the highway" way of responding, where the highway usually involves some form of violence, genocide, or annihilation of the "other." Or there is the co-existence model, which is a lot harder, because when you encounter something you don't understand and choose to sit in your discomfort taking the time and energy to learn about another way of being, your whole reality ends up changing because, holy crap, there is another way of being! It's much easier to just kill everyone else.

It is 2018 and we are still caught in this cycle. No wonder a majority of people of intelligence and goodwill in the West have rejected religion outright. I do not begrudge anyone who chooses not to be religious. I completely understand where they are coming from. I also believe them when they say they are "spiritual but not religious" and I in no way hold that against them. I wish the church would be more spiritual and less religious, if religious means close-minded, violent, intolerant, and basically doing more harm than good. If Jesus were to show up today I think he would hang out with the spiritual but not religious people. In fact, hanging out with the spiritual but not religious people is where I have recently found the most lifegiving community and transformational spiritual practices.

What about a third option in response to religious differences? What if we were able to both know who we are and learn from others—even allow your relationships with others to change who you are. What if we could be secure in our identity and hold that identity lightly enough that we are open to learning from how other people and other religions interact with God? Radical!

The "Out of the Box" Tool:

Sometimes we need tools to help us remember that God is bigger than any box we could ever put God in. As we grow and change, our relationship with God should also grow and change. Because we instinctively know this, I bet you have already explored various ways of encountering God that are not traditionally "Christian." Simply noticing, acknowledging, and validating this choice is important.

Here are a few example questions to notice the variety of your spiritual practices:

- Do you do yoga?
- Do you practice transcendental meditation or another kind of meditation?
- Have you developed your own rituals?
- Have you written your own prayers?

As Christian leaders we can fall into the trap of exclusively looking to our own traditions for spiritual resources or nourishment. When we do this, we cut ourselves off from so much potential spiritual growth and nourishment. That being said, when we engage with other cultures and traditions we must do so mindfully. It can be helpful to ask yourself questions to maintain a certain level of awareness and intentionality.

- Have you ever been exposed to another religion's or culture's way of encountering the Divine and tried it on for yourself?
- What was that experience like for you? Was it easy? Were you resistant?

- Did you struggle with concerns of appropriation?
- Did you find a teacher from that tradition to guide or teach you?
- Did you incorporate that practice into your spiritual repertoire?
- Did you determine a certain practice was not a good fit for you? If so, how did you come to that decision?

Checking In With God

So far, our discussion about your relationship with God has been kind of meta. Let's bring it down to earth, so to speak. As clergy, people can make a lot of assumptions about us and project their own assumptions, opinions and beliefs onto us. One of those assumptions is that we have a relationship with God. Not an outrageous assumption, given our profession. However, just because we have a relationship with God doesn't mean at this point in time it is a good or healthy relationship. And because relationships are always changing, just because we had a good relationship with God at one point provides no guarantees for what our relationship with God is like now.

Most people, including clergy, think if you become a minister then your relationship with God has received the stamp of approval lasting forever and always. Oh, if only it worked that way. Ministry can go a long way toward ruining one's relationship with God. In a bizarre twist of faith, the daily grind of being a priest can leave precious time to focus on one's relationship with God. Just like churches getting caught up in "doing church," clergy can get caught up in "doing ministry" and find they wake up one morning and can't remember the last time they prayed when they were not leading worship. And oh, the guilt! And the shame. So rather than admit this to ourselves, or a community of peer support, or even God, we ignore it and it only gets worse.

If you do not schedule time to check in with God it will not happen. If you do not prioritize your relationship with God, no one else will. Maintaining a healthy relationship with God is what the institutional church expects of us but does very little to support or encourage. We are told by our superiors to take our days off, go on retreats, make time for prayer and yet the culture of our churches and denominations remain breakneck. Given how vital they are to ministry, each of us should have had an entire class on boundaries in seminary. Instead, we have been left to figure out a mythical balance on our own.

Well, there is no hope of balance without God. Making a regular practice of simply checking in can go a long way.

The "Checking- in with God" Tool:

Taking stock of your relationship with God is a good thing to do now and then. Like your relationship with yourself, it can be a helpful barometer for your relationships in general. If it has been awhile and you are at a loss for where to begin, here are a few questions to get started:

- How do you know God loves you?
- When was the last time you and God directly communicated?
- When was the last time God surprised you?

- When was the last time you were really angry with God? Did you let God know? What happened then?
- When was the last time there was radio silence between you and God? What was that li
- When was the last time you just sat with God without talking?
- When was the last time you felt completely lit up inside? Was God there?

Okay, now I am going to ask you come up with some of your own markers for "evaluating" your relationship with God because one's relationship with God is an incredibly personal thing. So go ahead, check in with God. I'll wait.

In many ways it is fantastic that you have chosen and been chosen for a vocation where your relationship with God is so overtly a part of your job. In other ways it sucks, because, as I've said, the patriarchal world culture and the institutional church are less than stellar supports in encouraging their clergy to engage in the ongoing emotional work it takes to maintain healthy relationships, including our relationships with God. You would think this would be different. You would hope this would be different. Many people and places in the institutional church are trying to do this better. But if we want our clergy to survive their ministries, let alone thrive in them and fulfill their God-given purpose, major shifts are needed in order to prioritize the health and wholeness of our clergy's relationships—with themselves, with God, with their families and friends, and with creation. Things are not going to be different until we are different.

Alternative Spiritual Practices

Tactics and tools for rooting into your relationship with God abound. You already know a ton of them. You also already know what is more likely to work for you. I would even bet there is a practice you have wanted to try, that has been in the back of your mind for years, that seems like it could really work for you, but you have never gotten around to trying it. Now is the time! Even if it seems totally crazy but it speaks directly to that part of yourself inside of you where God lives—do it! Stop coming up with reasons "this is not how a priest connects to God" or "finds her truth," and listen to that still small voice inside of you. Which, coincidentally, is also exactly what the world needs from you right now, too.

It's not like this is your first rodeo. You know how to connect with God. It is your job, after all. Where you can get tripped up is maintaining that connection to God inside of you. How do I know this? Because everything in the world, including most of the stuff in our ministries, is set to throw that connection off course. When we get caught up in how our colleague disrespected us or how we are behind in our pledge drive or how Sunday's altar linens were wrinkled, we forget that our fundamental role as a person and a priest is to be a being in relationship with God. Since God is love, our job is to be in a relationship with Love, so that's pretty cool. If only it were easy to practice, let alone remember.

When we do remember this, we may still do all that other stuff, but we do it as a person who is in Love, which is a completely different version of ourselves.

She is the version we want to be. She is the one who said, "I think I am called to be a priest" and she is the one who knows exactly what that means. You dip in and out of her all the time. Now our task is to figure out what are the things you can focus on that will help you become her?

Tactics and tools for how to root into your relationship with God abound. You already know a ton of them. You also already know what is more likely to work for you. You know that thing you have wanted to try, that has been in the back of your mind for years, that seems like it could really work for you? Now is the time to try it! Or you know that thing, that has randomly shown up in your life, that seems like it is totally crazy, but it speaks *directly to that part of yourself inside where God lives?* Now is the time to do that thing! Now is the time to stop listening to every reason why "this is not how a priest connects to God" or "finds her truth" because it is exactly what you need right now. Which, coincidentally, is also exactly what the world needs from you right now, too.

This is not your first rodeo. You know how to connect with God. It's your job. Where you get tripped up is *maintaining* that connection to God *inside of you.* How do I know this? Because everything in the world, *including* most of the stuff in our ministries, is set to throw that connection off course. When we get caught up in how our colleague disrespected us or how we are behind in our pledge drive or how Sunday's altar linens were wrinkled, we forget that our fundamental identity is a being in relationship with Love.

When we remember this, we may still do all that stuff, but we do it as a person who *in Love,* which is a completely different version of ourselves. She is the version we want to be. She is the one who said, "I think I am called to be a priest" and she is the one who knows exactly what that means. You dip in and out of her all the time. What are the things you can focus on that will help you become her?

Stepping out in Faith

When I came to the end of the edge of the church, and decided to keep going, I signed up to work with Regena Thomashauer. You met her in the foreword. She is a power-house of a woman and she has become one of my greatest spiritual teachers. To say this was an unexpected develop-ment in my vocation would be an understatement. Her life's calling is helping women reconnect to their power by connecting to their bodies. While she does not always market it as such, Regena's work is totally spiritual. From the outside, her School of Womanly Arts, looks about as far away from the church as you can possibly get! But for me, working with her has helped me access the divinity in my body, which helped me access my power and my truth, which has transformed and deepened my relationship with God.

Who is your Regena? What is your School of Womanly arts? Is there a teacher you want to study with or a program you want to try that you have told yourself is "too out of the box" for you to participate in? Pay attention to that longing and explore that desire. Who knows what trans-formation awaits you if you follow that path! God can communicate with us in whatever way God wants. And if God keeps nudging you to try something "alternative," then try it. The worst thing that will happen is the practice won't be a good fit for you and you will move on. The best thing that could happen is that your relationship with God and yourself (and by extension all your relationships, including your ministry) will be deepened and transformed. Trust me, it is worth wading through any anxiety or sense of risk you might feel to get to that other side.

Grace

At this point in the book, you may have come to the realization that your relationship with yourself and/or your relationship with God are not what you want them to be. If this is the case, fear not. And please, please do not despair. You are not a lost cause. You have nothing to feel guilty about. As priests there is so much pressure on all of our relationships—our self, God, others. Sometimes, in order to cope we choose to pay less attention to our relationships because it is all just too painful and too hard. And because, on some level, this has been working for you, your brain's number one goal is to keep you doing the same thing! I get all bent out of shape with people who want to maintain the status quo, but this is how our brains are wired. Our brain's goal is to keep us alive. If we are still alive, our brain assumes what we are doing is working so we should keep doing it! But we also have a body, and a soul and a network of complex relationships. Luckily our brains can change and part of what we are doing hear is changing how we think so we can change how we feel so we can change what we do and change who we are. If you didn't believe people could change you would not be a priest. This priest is now telling you to extend that same belief to yourself.

Before you are a priest you are a person and God loves you, no matter what. At the end of the day, most of our struggles come down to whether we believe we are good enough or worthy of love. Does it feel like we have been here before? Because we have. We talked about this back in chapter three. If you struggle with self-worth and self-doubt, which many of us do, this can rear its head in our relationships with God. It will show up in all our relationships. It may be the biggest thing we are called to work on. Certainly, it is fundamental. It is also super hard. If some part of you is stuck here, it is ok. You are not alone. It is not even your fault. It is what you have learned. The good news is you can unlearn it. We can unlearn it together. You just have to be willing and you have to want it.

Shut Down the Shame

Because feeling not good enough or unlovable isn't enough, on top of this many of us will feel guilt or shame about feeling guilt and shame! Stop the madness! Ok, but how? Well, according to Brené Brown, and I trust everything that woman says, the way to combat shame is with empathy and self-compassion. The one, two punch! Or the one-arm, two-arms-wrap around-hug it out of 'em. In this case, you are hugging the shame out of yourself.

Awareness: Just like noticing when you are in disapproval of yourself and choosing to find yourself right—take away the guilt on top of guilt shame on top of shame. Neutralize that mess right now. Find yourself right.

Reach out. We are hardwired for connection. Find a friend, someone you trust, someone as Brené says, has earned the right to hear your story, and share with them. You are looking for empathy here. You can even tell them, "What I really need right now is for you to listen to me and then give me an empathic response." The act of seeking out someone to talk to is an act of self-compassion.

The "Send Yourself Light" Tool

When you notice yourself feeling shame, guilt, fear, self-doubt, unworthy, etc. try the following exercise:

- Notice where in your body you are having a physical sensation associated with an emotion or feeling.
- Place your attention on that area of your body. You can even place your hand there.
- Take a deep breath: inhale for a count of five, hold your breath for a count of five, exhale for a count of five, hold for a count of five. Repeat the entire process five times.
- As you are breathing imagine a warm, golden light filling the space in your body where the negative emotion resides.
- Imagine the warm, golden light spreading throughout your body until your entire body is filled. Then imagine the warm, golden light overflowing out of your body, out the top of your head, and running down the outside of your body, down to the earth.
- Take another five, deep, slow breaths.

God is a Woman

In my journey toward releasing a deeply ingrained sense of unworthiness and not enoughness, I had to challenge and let go of deeply held beliefs that were not serving my highest good. Like all of this work, it is a process. As clergy we know that we cannot make anyone believe that they are Beloved by God. All we can do is keep reminding them again and again of what is true and practice loving them. Same goes for ourselves. We have to practice loving ourselves before we believe we are lovable. We have to keep telling ourselves over and over again that we are loved until one day, something shifts. Something moves. Something is let go. It will happen for you, my dear. Keep working the tools. Keep showing up.

If in your exploration of "alternative spiritual practices" I highly recommend exploring the feminine divine. For those of us who have trouble believing, in the deepest recesses of our being, that we could possibly be worthy of God's love, expanding our view of the God that is doing the loving can be a helpful step in the process. As I said before, I had not previously been drawn to feminine expressions of the divine. In fact, I found those people, particularly female Christian ministers, who were all gaga over the Divine Feminine and Sophia and Wisdom to be a bit … weird. Why were they trying so hard? Why turn to something so… extreme? Well, after a decade of ministering in the patriarchal church, I now understand: everything is on the line for them – their faith, their relationship with God, their ministry, their bodies. If there is no room in our churches for a God who is feminine, how are we to believe there is room in our churches for ministers who are feminine?

Never in a million years would I have expected to resonate with references to the divine as "Goddess." In fact, at first it was really, really hard for me. Whenever I read or heard the word "Goddess" I always translated it in my head to "God." Eventually I asked myself, "Why do I need to make her Goddess my God?"

Intellectually I knew that the church sanctioned image of "God the Father" exercises powerful control over all of us and intuitively I knew this was limiting and oppressive. I just chose to believe it was a necessary tradeoff for remaining in the fold of the institutional church. But the more experiences I had where I felt the church did not value me as much because I was not a man, the more I resented the instruction and mandate to worship a male God. Now, in order to pray the prayer, "God our Father," I willingly disconnect from the part of myself that is wounded by those words. I am becoming more unable and unwilling to do this. Rather than lamenting my lack of courage to commit to never saying them ever again, as I know some women have, I choose to find myself right and I extend myself grace. A more inclusive and whole image for God will require something from all of us.

To restore or reinvigorate your relationship with God, you may need to search beyond the church, or deep within the recesses of her history, to find ways of connecting to God that are radical enough to give you life. The spirit of God is wild and free, just like a woman. Thousands of years of patriarchy have done much to clip our wings. No one is going to give us permission to seek the healing we need. No one is going to do this work for us. If we want to reclaim our passionate relationship with the Divine then we have to pursue her and follow wherever she leads. I'm warning you now, you may be surprised where this journey takes you and it could very well lead to the ride of your life.

The Hang Out with the Goddess Tool:

Goddess is simply the feminine form of God. That's all. In the privacy of your own home, in the seclusion of your own brain, spend some time thinking about her.

- Who is she?
- What does she look like?
- How does she move in the world?
- If you get curious about how others have conceived of her over the centuries, try reading *Goddesses: Mysteries of the Feminine Divine* by Joseph Campbell and Safron Elsabeth Rossi.
- Dabble with using "Goddess" rather than "God" from time to time. You don't have to do it during the liturgy, just in your own prayer time or when conversing with friends about the Divine. If "Goddess" feels like too much try "Mother" or "Mater" or "Sophia."
- Notice what you feel and question the messages your feelings are trying to give you.

Mary Daly has famously said, "If God is male then male is God." The implications of this on our ministries and ourselves cannot be overstated. We may spend the rest of our lives unlearning and unpacking the damage the exclusive worship of a male God has done to our psyches and souls – not just as women, but as people.

To become the priests God is calling us to be, we must realize that our gender is not something to overcome or erase, but something to celebrate and affirm. Knowing God as Goddess has the potential to crack something open inside of a woman and give her access to a part of herself she always knew was there part of God she has always know was there, but could never quite reach before.

Just try it. If you hate it, stop. But if it cracks you open, don't be afraid. She's got you.

CHAPTER 6

Your Relationships with Others

———— ◆ ————

"We are born in relationship, we are wounded in relationship, and we can be healed in relationship. Indeed, we cannot be fully healed outside of relationship."

– Harville Hendrix,
Getting the Love You Want

Save the Drama for Your Mama

"I don't know exactly what this means yet, but I want to create something new." I was sitting in a café in Baltimore with my friend the Rev. Jennifer DiFrancessco and I was sharing with her how frustrated and restless I was becoming in my ministry. Jenn and I knew each other from the neighborhood—our churches were only a few blocks apart and we had collaborated on things like Vacation Bible School, special worship services, and other community events. Jenn looked up, starred right at me, and said, "I feel the same way."

She and I, along with the Rev. Jason Chesnut, would go on to co-create a "new thing" called the Slate Project. A huge impetus for co-founding this alternative Christian community was our shared desire to create a different way of being in relationships with our ministry colleagues and with the members of our community. We all had had similar relational struggles and we wanted to figure out a way to do things differently. Starting from scratch had its advantages. But we soon learned that whenever you have relationships with other people, you will have conflict.

"Duh," you might be thinking. But this was a huge learning for me. I realized then that if I spent the rest of my ministry running from conflict, I would be constantly leaving to go to a new place. Alternatively, I could take the popular approach staying put yet avoiding conflict, but that did not sit well with me either. I have a propensity for telling the truth. Occasionally, it gets me in trouble. In my opinion, it is a least the right kind of trouble. Jenn, Jason and I decided we were committed to each other and committed to our community enough to do the difficult work of having difficult conversations. I'm sure there were times they were sick of me saying, "Guys, can we talk? I don't think we are on the same page." There were certainly times I got sick of myself and my continual need to talk things through rather than ignore what was going on. In those moments, Jenn and Jason would say, "No, this is important. Let's talk."

I'm going to go out on a limb and guess that relationships with other people may play a role in the frustrations you have with your current ministry and the institutional church. I know, I'm psychic. Volumes of books have been written about relationships – how to have them, how to fix them, what's wrong with them, what's right about them, tools, tricks, trades, I'm exhausted already. In this chapter I am going to introduce you to a few of my very favorite tools, practices, and resources I have discovered that have helped improve, not just my relationships with others, but my relationships, period – because remember, they are all interconnected.

Communication is Key

Relationships are 90 percent communication. I just made that up, but it sounds legit doesn't it? One of my coaches, Dr. Angela Lauria, says that success in life is 10 percent strategy, 10 percent tactics, and 80 percent "managing the drama." Effective and healthy communication plays a major role in managing the drama. We have already talked about ways of improving your communication with yourself and with God to improve those relationships. Now we are going to spend some time becoming familiar with tools for communicating with others, so we can not only better manage the drama, we can be the church.

One of the most helpful tools I have encountered for communicating honestly and effectively, where the roles of both speaker and listener are equally engaged, is a tool called the Imago Dialogue Process. Originally created by Dr. Harville Hendrix and Helen LaKelly Hunt as communication tool for romantic partners, I have found it works well to improve and strengthen the communication and overall relationship between any two people. This chapter is a bit different than the rest. Because communication plays such a huge role in our relationships with others I am going to spend a large portion of this chapter walking you through the Imago Dialogue tool and how to use it. As you master this tool you will have a brand new superpower to use in service of the art of feminine spiritual leadership.

Imago Dialogue

One of the most helpful tools I have encountered for communicating honestly and effectively, where the roles of both speaker and listener are equally engaged, is a tool called the Imago Dialogue Process. Originally created by Dr. Harville Hendrix and Helen LaKelly Hunt as communication tool for romantic partners, I have found it works well to improve and strengthen the communication and overall relationship between any two people.

The "Imago Dialogue" Tool:

Here are the basics of how the dialogue works:

1. One person initiates the conversation by "making an appointment" – literally saying to the other person, "I would like to dialogue about (fill in the blank). Is now a good time?"

   - In this step, the person initiating the conversation is clear that they have something they want to dialogue about and asks permission to begin the dialogue.

   - The person receiving the invitation to dialogue can respond either, "Yes, now is a good time" or "No, let's schedule a better time."

   - If it is a good time, the initiator continues. If it is *not* a good time, the two people schedule a time that works for both of them to have the dialogue.

- In the beginning, this way of communicating may feel awkward or forced. We are not used to stating our requests to converse so clearly! The more you practice this way of dialoging, the more natural it will feel.

- Already the dialogue has begun in a way where both people are being considerate and respectful of one another, setting a good foundation for the continued dialogue.

2. Next, the Sender (the person who initiated the dialogue) states the topic of the dialogue in one sentence.

- This requires the Sender to be focused, concise, and clear about what they wish to dialogue about.

- Clear communication requires thoughtfulness and intention. This step reminds us to take the time to be clear and focused in what we wish to communicate before we start speaking speaking. in an effort to avoid miscommunication and the resulting negative outcomes including hurt feelings, etc.

3. This is the first opportunity for the Receiver (the person receiving the request to dialogue) to practice one of the key tools in the Imago Dialogue: "mirroring." Mirroring is simply the process of mirroring back what you have understood the other person to have said and checking out your assumptions to see if what you heard is indeed what the Sender intended to communicate.

- When mirroring the Receiver can use a phrase such as, "Let me see if I've got it. You said ... "and then they repeat back what they heard the other person say.

- For example, it might go something like: "Let me see if I've got it. You said you want to dialogue about how well we are sticking to our home renovation budget." Then the Receiver would end with, "Is that right?" at which point the Sender will say, "Yes, that's right" and continue or "No, that's not quite it" and will rephrase the topic they desire to dialogue about. Then the Receiver would mirror again, until the Sender confirms they got it right.

- Mirroring is an incredibly useful tool for ensuring that each person in the conversation feels clearly heard and understood. Used consistently, it has the power to drastically reduce miscommunications. Rather than making assumptions about what you think another person means, even about something fairly clear, mirroring back to them what you heard allows you to check in with the other person to make sure you know exactly what they are saying.

4. Once the topic has been identified, the heart of the conversation can begin. Using "I" language, the Sender sends a message to convey her thoughts, feelings, or experiences to the Receiver.

- While the message may contain negative emotions, there may be no accusations or "You ..." statements. For example: "You make me feel stupid when you yell at me for forgetting to take out the trash."

- The Sender must speak about themselves not the other person using sentiments like, "I feel," "I love," I need," etc. For example, "I feel loved when you call me out of the blue just to say, 'Hi.'"
- It is important for the Sender to send messages in small amounts so the Receiver can hear them and be able to repeat them back. The Sender should say a few sentences and then pause so the Receiver can mirror back what they heard. If the Sender is going on for too long, the Receiver can ask them to, "Please pause," so the Receiver can mirror back what has been said, and then the Sender can resume speaking.

5. After each pause, the Receiver then mirrors back what the Sender has just said.

- The Receiver can use phrases like, "Let me see if I've got you" or "I heard you say..." to mirror back what they heard.
- Then they ask for confirmation by saying, "Is that right?" or "Did I get that?"
- Again, the Sender has the opportunity here to say, "Yes, you got it" or "No, you did not quite get it."
- If the Receiver *did get* the mirroring right, they invite the Sender to keep sharing by saying, "Is there more about that?" If there is more, the Sender can share again, in small amounts.
- If the Receiver says, "Is there more?" and the sender says, "No, that is all," now the Receiver moves on to the next step.

6. Once the Sender has finished sharing, the Receiver does a "summary mirror" where they go back and mirror everything that the Sender has said and at the end they say, "Did I get it?"

- This is where the active listening and the constant mirroring back pays off. It might seem daunting to try and summarize all that a person has said to you, but because you have been actively listening, mirroring back, and checking in with the accuracy of your information gathering, it is not as hard as it seems – but it is real work!

- When the Receiver finishes they ask, "Did I get it?" The Sender has the opportunity to share anything they felt the Receiver missed in their summary. This can be helpful because when a person is listening to another person it is possible to miss or overlook something that was said that may not have seemed important to the Receiver but was in fact very important to the Sender! The summary mirroring step allows for those mistakes to be corrected in the moment.

7. Once the Receiver has provided the summary mirror the next step in the Dialogue process is validation. In addition to listening fully to the Sender, the Receiver stretches to understand and acknowledge the validity of the Sender's point of view. This is especially important when the Sender's point of view is different than the Receivers. The heart of validation is the acknowledgement that the Sender's point of view "makes sense."

The Receiver doesn't have to hold the same view as the Sender or even agree with it, but they are required to stretch their empathy and understanding to acknowledge that whatever the Sender has just expressed makes sense *for them*.

- The Receiver provides validation by saying something like "What you have said makes sense because ..." and then the Receiver finds something about what the Sender said that truly makes sense to them.

8. The final step of the Imago Dialogue process is empathy. During the dialogue, the Receiver and the Sender have been creating an imaginary bridge between them. In this step, the Receiver steps over the imaginary bridge into the Sender's world and tries to imagine what they are feeling about the issue they are dialoguing about. In conversations we often assume we know what the other person is feeling. Attempting to "put yourself in the other person's shoes" and feel empathy is one of the key ways we build healthy relationships with one another. But in this step, the Receiver checks out their assumptions and asks the Sender directly if they are in fact feeling those feelings.

- The Receiver says something like, "I imagine what you might be feeling over this issue is ..." and then concludes with "Did I get it right?"
- Then, as usual, the Receiver allows the Sender to correct any suggestions that are not accurate and to add anything that might be missing. There is no need to feel any guilt or anxiety about "getting it wrong"

when trying to imagine how the other person is feeling. This entire process is about learning and checking out our assumptions from a place of love. If you engage in the process with love, there is no getting it wrong.

- As you use this Dialogue Process more and more, each person is able to move beyond their own limited experience of the other person based on their guesses and perceptions of what the other person may be feeling and thinking, toward an ability to experience the other person's internal reality as they choose to share it with them.

Ta da! That was a lot! You likely already knew how to use the tools of mirroring, validating and showing empathy for another person but the genius of this dialogue process is that it provides a structure where these tools can work together and a way of practicing them together so that they consistently build on one another to create clearer and stronger communication.

While it is very helpful when both people have been introduced to the Imago Dialogue process, it is not necessary for the person you are communicating with to know the dialogue process in order for you to utilize many of its techniques. You can use the key phrases to practice mirroring, validating, and empathy in any conversation. Using this tool can help us to learn to participate in the emotional realm of another person, while at the same time holding onto our own, separate experiences.

It can be difficult to build relationships of trust and understanding with people with whom you have fundamental disagreements. However, you do not have to agree with another person in order to express empathy for them or to understand how their position makes sense to them – even if it does not make sense to you! Given how polarized much of our world feels these days, having a tool to help communicate and listen from a place of empathy is incredibly valuable.

All people deeply desire to be both seen and heard. This is why the practice of giving one's spiritual "testimony" can be so powerful. Our stories are expressions of who we are. When we feel safe enough to share our personal stories with one another our relationships are deepened and strengthened. Validating another person's experience goes a long way toward building trust. Creating the space where another person feels (1) invited to share and (2) comfortable *enough* to share is another superpower women have that we rarely recognize as a superpower. In the feminine spiritual arts this tool is known as "Creating a Sacred Container."

The "Creating a Sacred Container" Tool:

Creating a sacred container is less of a process and more of an art, so I will describe how it can be done rather than lay it out in steps.

Poet and activist Sonya Renee Taylor says in her book The Body is Not an Apology: The Power of Radical Self-Love, "When we hear someone's truth and it strikes some deep part of our humanity, our own hidden shames, it can be easy to recoil into silence. We struggle to hold the truths of others because we so rarely have experienced having our own truths held." Women have a powerful ability to hold space for one another's truths.

Practicing the art of feminine spiritual leadership involves practicing awareness of the subtle shifts in energy both in people and between people. When we "Create a Sacred Container," we start by responding to an awareness in ourselves that notices and knows something needs to happen, something needs to be shared; it could be something between you and another person, between a person and themselves, or between a group of people.

Sacred containers have intentional openings, or beginnings, middles and endings or closings. These stages are essential to the stability and safety of the container. Your job is to indicate to others that the container is being put in place. You give voice to what you have sensed – that something desires to be expressed or attended to. You then invite the other person or persons into the container where this work can be done. You cannot force another person into a sacred container, you can only provide the invitation and hold the space.

If the invitation is accepted, then your job is to outline the parameters of the container and see if they are acceptable for everyone involved. This can include inviting those present to adhere to certain norms for and ways of communicating. By clearly describing what is acceptable and what is not acceptable behavior in the container you give the container structure. You are also solidifying yourself as a key space holder and inviting others into the posture of space holding with you – collectively, everyone together makes the sacred container.

Then you may invite whatever needs to be said, done, experienced, or shared to happen in that time and space. Leading liturgy is an example of creating a sacred container. We have been trained in how to hold sacred space during a liturgy. But what about during a counseling session or in a committee meeting? Every time human beings gather together, there is the potential for a sacred container to be created where all kinds of relational work can be done. Creating strong sacred containers is a skill we can develop and practice to become more adept at.

Every person can sense energy – some are more attuned to energy than others. Energy is another word for Spirit. When you sense what is going on inside another person you are sensing their energy. When you are in a large room full of people and you sense the "feeling" in the room change, you are sensing the energy change. We are sensing and responding to energy in ourselves and in others (and in nature!) all the time. You know how you can walk outside and it "feels" like rain before it has started to rain? You are sensing the atmospheric energy. Being "sensitive" is a feminine spiritual leadership superpower! Name it and claim it, baby! One way to use this power is by holding space.

Once whatever has needed to happen has happened in the container, then you must close it. You will be able to sense the energy in the room and in the people who are with you. Follow the natural progression of the energy. Allow things to finish when they desire to be finished. All the work will not be done – all the work will never be done! What was able to be accomplished will have been accomplished and by closing the container you give everyone a sense of completion that will allow them to move from that space feeling safe, secure, and good about what occurred. If you don't close the container, things will feel "left open" or "unresolved." Even if everything is *not resolved,* acknowledging that and saying that we have finished what we can do *right now* will allow people to leave that container and move forward feeling much better about what happened.

At some point later it can be helpful to reflect on the experience of what took place in the container, with the same people who experienced it or with others. Taking time later to reflect and to process helps to solidify any healing that took place in the container as well as identify any next steps that could be or should be taken. Creating sacred containers for conversations is one of our greatest abilities and one of our greatest roles as ministers. There are times when "conversation" is not what needs to happen in the container but silence, or song, or movement. Trust your intuition and check out your assumptions with others so you can discern together the best way to create and utilize the container.

The Desire to Be Seen and Known

All communication is motivated, on some level, by a desire to be heard and understood. The Imago Dialogue Process as a whole and the individual techniques it teaches help us to communicate with one another in a way that says, "I care about you. I respect you. I want to know you. And I want you to know me." This simple message can go so far toward managing and even eliminating drama in relationships with others. Creating sacred containers is a way to intentionally invite people to an experience where they can engage in the elements of relationship for which they long. People are invited to show up as their full selves, no parts are excluded or shamed; people are invited to speak their deepest truths aloud and be heard, perhaps for the first time ever; people experience being known and loved for who they are, no questions; people have reflected back to them their own divinity and catch a glimpse of who they truly are in the eyes of another person; people have a concrete experience of loving one another the way God loves us – unconditionally, with no judgment, freely given.

If you doubt that the sacred containers you create have this type of power, think about a time when you were invited into a sacred container by someone else – a time you were held in love by a group of people who gave you the space to be, in that moment, everything you are and everything you aren't. Did you feel God's love in that moment? Can you still remember *exactly* what it felt like? As Maya Angelou said, people will forget what you said, but they will never forget how you made them feel.

Healing happens in sacred containers. As clergy, we have the privilege of helping them pop up anytime, anywhere. Feminine spiritual leaders are conscious of when they are creating sacred containers and they realize the responsibility that comes with creating and tending to them. Not everyone can do this or do it well. Learning how to do it well and being committed to becoming better and better at it is a feminine spiritual leadership art and a very bad*ss priest thing to do, indeed.

CHAPTER 7

Your Relationship with All of Creation/The Cosmos

———— ◆ ————

"The universe is the primary revelation of the divine, the primary scripture, the primary locus of divine-human communion."

– THOMAS BERRY

Better Than Dominion

If this book had a tag line it would be "It's all about relationships." I often like to tack on the descriptors of those relationships as being "with ourselves, each other, God, and all of creation." As Christians, this should not be hard to get behind. We believe humans are part of the created order and that God is the creator of all things. But how much do we think about our *relationship* with creation? How important is our relationship with creation in our day-to-day lives?

To be honest, having a conscious relationship with creation is a new thing for me. Of all my relationships it is the one that feels most foreign and difficult. To have a relationship with creation is an unusual concept to most western Christians – the effect of many centuries of separating matter and spirit in our understanding. My own growth in the art of feminine spiritual leadership has included unlearning unhelpful ways of thinking and being that no longer serve and are no longer true. One of the biggest things I am unlearning is the belief that I am disconnected from all that is and that humanity is disconnected from the rest of creation.

Traditional Christian understanding of humanity's relationship with creation has been to view our relationship with creation as one of dominion over or stewardship of. This viewpoint has often been labeled the "biblical" view of creation. A quick and *close* reading of Genesis 1:26 shows that technically God gives humans "dominion" "over the fish of the sea, and over the birds of the air, and over the cattle, and over all the wild animals of the earth, and over "every creeping thing that creeps upon the earth." This is by no means *all* of creation. Also, the concept of "dominion" has to do with ruling over but in no way implies the greed, exploitation, or destruction that has characterized must of humanity's relationship with the earth. And yet many have argued the word "dominion" (*radah* in Hebrew) basically gives humanity a pass to do whatever we want to creation – an argument that is in no way "biblical" let alone anywhere close to theologically sound. But there is not destroying creation and then there is having a healthy relationship with it.

To take a grand concept to an even grander scale, we can stretch our imaginations to think about our relationship not just to all of creation, but the entire cosmos.

When I think of creation I think of the earth and the beings who inhabit it. When I think of *the cosmos,* I think of the entire universe. In the Episcopal Church we have a Eucharistic Prayer (Prayer C) that uses language that expresses what I'm trying to get at here. The prayer speaks of how at God's command "all things came to be: the vast expanse of interstellar space, galaxies, suns, the planets in their courses" – that's pretty cosmic stuff! The prayer goes on to say God also brought into being, "this fragile earth, our island home." By God's will both creation and the cosmos were "created and have their being."

Everything Is Connected

Although uncommon, the idea that God has a relationship with creation and with the cosmos is not foreign to our faith. But what is *our* relationship to them? And if traditional Christian understandings of our relationship to creation have been lacking, how do we discern what a healthier and more whole relationship with the cosmos might look like? Even Eucharistic Prayer C says that God made humanity "rulers of creation" but did God, really? What if our relationship with creation was always meant to be more connected and interconnected than we have realized?

Scientists and climatologists are screaming at the top of their lungs for the world to recognize just how much damage we have already done to the planet. They are begging us to change our ways in an attempt to save not only the earth, but ourselves! This is the only planet we have.

There is no plan B. Even if at some point refugees from earth take off for another planet, our existence and our future are connected to the future of the *universe*. Our universe. Our planet. From God's perspective, we might belong more to earth than earth belongs to us – who knows!

It can be hard to wrap our heads around the fact that each of us, as human beings, are like one drop of water in the vast ocean that is humanity, and our entire planet is like one grain of sand in the desert that is the universe. How can we ever comprehend just how small we are and at the same time that we are as valued and loved as every other speck of matter that makes up the universe? All matter matters to God – talk about a great equalizer! And all matter comes from the great Mater or Mother of us all.

The practice of paying attention to my relationship with the Universe helps me to put my life in perspective – I am both exquisitely not in control and, in the grand scheme of things, I am not that important, *and at the same time,* what I do matters on the grandest of scales because it matters *to God.* Like the butterfly effect – everything is connected. I don't have to understand how it all works to know it is true. I don't have to see it all unfolding to connect to The Unfolding.

All Things Necessary?

I used to think there were certain things that were off limits to me as a priest. Like there were certain spiritual practices or ways of thinking about the world that were too woo-woo for a minister of the church to dabble in, especially in public! Before I took my ordination vows,

I seriously had to ask myself if I truly believed the Holy Scriptures of the Old and New Testaments to contain all things necessary to salvation – a phrase I was required to consent to in my ordination. A friend of mine, who is also an Episcopal priest, pointed out to me it does not say those things necessary for salvation are *only* contained in the Old and New Testament. I promise I was not trying to game my ordination vows. But as spiritual beings in the twenty-first century, it is time we get past the belief that our path is the only path to God.

I bring all this up in this section about your relationship with the universe because this might be an opportunity to explore what other spiritual traditions have had to say on the subject. It also might be the place to expand your Christian influences and look into Christian cosmology, ecojustice theologies, etc. There has never been a time when Christians did not take from other cultures and religious traditions and incorporate them into their own practices and beliefs.

Healthy relationships, by design, involve give and take. Refusing to be affected or influenced by our neighbors who practice other religions and spiritualties is a byproduct of our overall refusal to be in relationship with people who are different, simply because we fear what we don't know. We fear what we don't know and we don't know what we don't understand and we don't understand what we don't engage with – this is the case with people and it is the case with the cosmos. The deceptively simple choice is to engage even if we are afraid, to choose a moment of discomfort over a life stuck in fear. These choices are the art of feminine spiritual leadership at work and they have the power to change the world.

Awakening to Cosmic Relationality

John Philip Newell, former warden of Iona Abbey and an ordained Church of Scotland minister, has written extensively on the subject of humanity's relationship with the cosmos in his book *A New Harmony: The Spirit, the Earth, and the Human Soul*. There he says,

"The word kosmos in ancient Greek means 'a harmony of parts.' In the classical world, everything in the universe was viewed as moving in relation to everything else. This ancient understanding of the cosmos is being born afresh today in radically new ways. We are realizing that the whole of reality is one. In nearly every dimension of life – whether economic or religious, scientific or political – there is a growing awareness of earth's essential interrelatedness. This new-ancient way of seeing is radically challenging us to see ourselves as connected with everything that exists. And it means that any true vision of reality must also be a cosmology, a way of relating the parts to the whole, of seeing our distinct journeys in relation to the one journey of the universe."

How do we go about making this cosmological relationality a part of our everyday lives? Is it even possible to have a relationship with the cosmos or with creation that is comparable to our relationship with our friends, family, or even God? A good place to start is getting to know creation better. Perhaps spending more time together. Have you ever noticed a desire within yourself to spend more time in nature or to get outside more? It is like our bodies know when it has been too long between visits. Like everything, it starts with attention and awareness. Once we realize we desire more connection with the creation, it helps to remember that our relationship with creation is not separate from any of our other relationships. Otherwise trying to improve your relationship with creation can feel a bit daunting. Remember, you are not starting from zero. A place to start could be noticing how you are already connected.

Practice Being in the Flow

Perhaps you have always felt a strong connection to the water – you could explore that connection.

- Consider that you already have a relationship with water.
- Why is that relationship important to you?
- What does that relationship give you?
- Are there ways you are being called to engage with water as a part of creation?

The perennial wisdom traditions of all faiths have recognized humanity's innate connection to creation. Ancient masters taught their pupils to be steadfast and supple, like water – flowing rather than fixed, rigid, or static. Eventually, water's constant flow will wear down anything in its path and simply carry it away. Practice "getting in the flow" by imagining yourself to be made up of the same stuff as water. You are just as powerful, just as capable of calm beauty and raging force. When you are connected to your flow, in your flow, you control the flow.

Finding ways to connect to the earth will depend on your geographical location, your access, your preferences, etc. As you feel into this, I encourage you to press your edges. If you have never felt like an "outdoor person," ask yourself why and spend some time sitting with that question. This is also an opportunity to reconnect to creation in ways you may have been previously drawn to but have not engaged with in a while. Did you used to enjoy hiking in the forest, but you can't remember the last time you did that? Plan to go and this time practice connecting to the trees, the air, the animals with a spiritual and relational reverence. Tune in and notice what you find.

The "Making Right the Path" Tool:

There is so much room to explore in our relationships with creation and working on these relationships is so necessary. At this point in human history, when we are disconnected from so much, perhaps nothing is so severe as our disconnection from creation. We have lost part of ourselves with this lost connection, so much so we don't even know what we don't know. Pay attention to any longings you feel as you explore reconnecting to creation. There are wounds within us that need to be healed and there are a vast array of resources we have for healing. Some of them belong to our own Christian tradition. I have found the practice of confessing my own personal neglect and negligence for the care of creation, as well as our collective wrongs against the earth, to be very powerful. This has come from a profound need to repent and ask forgiveness from the earth herself, not just from God.

At first, I would pray this prayer when I stopped to pick up trash on the beach. Then I thought to pray it each time I drove my car and added carbon dioxide and other greenhouse gasses to the atmosphere. Unfortunately, there are many opportunities to be reminded of the ways we abuse our planet and her resources. Because it was becoming too depressing to simply pray a prayer of confession over and over, I decided I need to pair it with a prayer of thanksgiving and renewed relationship. What came to me was a prayer some refer to as the *Ho'oponopono* Prayer, which is often attributed to Hawaiian spirituality. Popular (westernized) versions of the prayer usually go something like this: "I'm sorry. Please forgive me. Thank you. I love you." Not wanting to appropriate or misattribute this prayer I spoke to a *Kumu* (traditional Hawaiian teacher) with whom I work and asked him if it would be appropriate to use the prayer in this way. He said that Ho'oponopono is not actually a prayer but a form of meditation.

Morrnah Nalamaku Simeona was the creator of the modern use of Ho'oponopono. A native Hawaiian *Kahuna Lapa'ua* (Kahuna means "keeper of the secret" and *Lapa'au* means "a specialist in healing"). She was chosen to be a *kahuna* while still a small child, and she was given the gift of healing at the tender age of three. Morrnah took her knowledge of the ancient spiritual cleansing ritual and created a modernized process, where rather than depending on the presence of a *kahuna* or priest to conduct the ritual, any individual person could engage in the Ho'oponopono practice. She traveled the world promoting and teaching her revised process and philosophy, which she called *Self I-Dentity through Ho'oponopono* (*SITH*). In 1980 she founded the organization *Foundation of I, Inc. (Freedom of the Cosmos)* for the purpose of preserving, promoting, and maintaining the integrity of her spiritual teachings, as well as for teaching instructors the *SITH* self-realization process so they, in turn, could teach others.

The word *Ho'oponopono* means to make right, to rectify an error. Morrnah described the process as a way to "appeal to Divinity who knows our personal blueprint, for healing of all thoughts and memories that are holding us back at this time.... It is a matter of going beyond traditional means of accessing knowledge about ourselves." The main purpose of the Ho'oponopono process is to discover the divinity within one's self and develop a relationship with that divinity – which was our focus in the last chapter!

By focusing on developing a working relationship with divinity within one's self, the Ho'oponopono process invites us to learn to ask in each moment how we have errored in thought, word, deed, or action and allows us to release that energy so our memories and relationships may be cleansed.

Humanity's relationship with the *'aina* (land) needs to be cleansed. My relationship with the land needs to be cleansed. *The Foundation of I, Inc.* has included the following two prayers on their website for public use. I encourage you to use them in the spirit of Ho'oponopono, "making right more right, the path."

"I" AM THE "I"

(OWAU NO KA "I")

"I" come forth from the void into light,

Pua mai au mai ka po iloko o ka malamalama,

"I" am the breath that nurtures life,

Owau no ka ha, ka mauli ola,

*"I" am that emptiness, that hollowness
beyond all consciousness,*

Owau no ka poho, ke ka'ele mawaho a'e o no ike apau.

The "I," the Id, the All.

Ka "I," Ke Kino Iho, na Mea Apau.

"I" draw my bow of rainbows across the waters,

*Ka a'e au "I" ku'u pi'o o na anuenue mawaho
a'e o na kai a pau,*

The continuum of minds with matters.

Ka ho'omaumau o na mana'o ame na mea a pau.

"I" am the incoming and outgoing of breath,

Owau no ka "Ho" a me ka "Ha,"

The invisible, untouchable breeze,

He huna ka makani nahenahe,

The undefinable atom of creation.

Ka "Hua" huna o Kumulipo.

"I" am the "I."

Owau no ka "I."

THE PEACE OF "I"

(KA MALUHIA O KA "I")

Peace be with you, All My Peace,

O ka Maluhia no me oe, Ku'u Maluhia a pau loa,

The Peace that is "I," the Peace that is "I am."

Ka Maluhia o ka "I," owau no ka Maluhia,

The Peace for always, now and forever and evermore.

Ka Maluhia no na wa a pau, no ke'ia
wa a mau a mau loa aku.

My Peace "I" give to you, My Peace "I" leave with you,

Ha'awi aku wau "I" ku'u Maluhia ia oe, waiho aku wau
"I" ku'u Maluhia me oe,

Not the world's Peace, but, only My Peace,

The Peace of "I."

A'ole ka Maluhia o ke ao aka, ka'u Maluhia wale no,

Ka Maluhia o ka "I."

Healing the Mother Earth Wound

The earth is very forgiving *and* she will not cease to hold us accountable for our actions. She has a bigger picture to keep in mind. We must re-learn our place in the flow of all things. There are answers to how we are being called to move forward, particularly in relationship to how to exist more responsibly and sustainably on the earth. Answers the earth desires to give us. I know that may sound weird, but I feel she is trying to tell us things we deeply need to know.

One thing in my life I have never been able to rationally explain is my deep attraction to and love for Hawaii. Ever since I was a little girl I have been obsessed with Hawaii and felt an intense longing, not just to visit, but to *be* there. I can't explain it. As far as I know my ancestors are not from this part of the world. But a part of my soul has always known this is home. I visited for the first time when I was eighteen years old and seventeen years later I moved to Maui. As I write this the rain is falling in Kula, the town where I live in on the slopes of Haleakala Mountain (which is also a volcano!). I can sense the rain with each of my senses – I heard it before I saw it, I can smell its freshness and feel it cooling the air by several degrees in only a few minutes. Right now, I just had to go outside and let it fall all over my skin, down my face, and into my mouth. Maui has called me to her; I feel that this land has invited me here to heal. I honestly have no idea what that means but I believe it with all of my being.

The earth is calling to us. Creation is calling to us. She wants us to heal. Our healing is inextricably linked to Her healing. There will not, there cannot be one without the other. We are infants when it comes to learning what this all means. So, we take baby steps like going outside to stand in the rain, when you feel the call to go outside and stand in the rain. Noticing how the air is cooler now than it was five minutes ago. Listing to that longing inside and noticing when the longing is speaking directly to your connection with creation – because that longing is evidence of the relationship. As priests, we are so lucky. We already know about calling and discernment and feelings and longings. We know what that is, we know how to listen, we know how to respond. We know how to trust that this is *real* and not our imaginations or a coincidence or too "woo-woo." This is as real as it gets.

Each relationship we invest in and strengthen builds on our other connections. The work you do to love and care for yourself will increase your ability to love and care for others. The more you practice awareness of your relationship with God the more you will recognize God in creation and *creation in God*. It is all the same stuff, the same love, the same connection, the same. And when one of these relationships gets neglected, they are all affected. The neglect effect can be just as powerful. The amazing thing is that even the subtlest shifts of awareness and intention can have the biggest ramifications. In some ways it doesn't take much at all, just a small shift, like opening your eyes. It is the difference between seeing and being completely in the dark.

CHAPTER 8

Feeling Is Your Superpower

———— ◆ ————

"This being human is a guest house. Every morning
a new arrival. A joy, a depression, a meanness, some
momentary awareness comes as an unexpected visitor.
Welcome them all. The dark thought, the shame, the
malice, meet then at the door laughing and invite
them in. Be grateful for whoever comes because each
has been sent as a guide from beyond."

– RUMI

I'm Fine!

"Tell me a story from your childhood." My wife Heather
and I were driving from our home in Baltimore to visit her
family in Connecticut, and after a few hours the conversation had lulled. She was driving. I was falling asleep. I think
she was bored.

"Tell me a story!" she said again, this time more insis-
tently. My mind was blank. I could not think of anything.
"I don't have any stories!" I said, realizing as I said that how
ridiculous it sounded, but I seriously could not think of "a
story" from my childhood to tell her. A story – a tale with
a beginning, middle, and end, with a point or a moral or

something interesting in there that made it worthy of the breath it took to give it voice. Something worth listening to. What the heck! Why could I not think of anything?

In that moment, I realized I had spent a lot of time and energy training myself not to allow experiences from my past to take up any space in my brain. It is not that I had a terrible childhood. By most accounts it was completely normal. Boring, even. Fine. Ah, *fine*. (You know what fine stands for? F*cked-up, Insecure, Neurotic and Emotional. Just ask Aerosmith.) Clearly I had *feelings* about my childhood, evidenced by the fact I could not readily access much of anything from that time in my life, which gave me great pause.

Heather told me stories about her childhood all the time. Not great epic tales like the Odyssey, but occasionally something would happen that would trigger a memory from when she was a kid and she would share it with me. It was as simple and uneventful as that. And yet that rarely if ever happened to me. I realized not only did Heather not know much about my childhood because I never spontaneously shared things with her, but I had, over time, cut myself off from any kind of close connection with my past. I don't think I had gone so far as to repress these memories, but I did not keep them readily at hand, so to speak. They were deep within me, buried, far away, long ago, not worth mentioning.

Why? Well, when Heather said, "Tell me a story from your childhood," I did think of something. I thought of something immediately. It was my most vivid memory from childhood and it was super easy to recall. But it was not a story I wanted to casually tell on a five-hour car ride to Connecticut. It was not just a story, it was a box I did not want to open.

What We Do to Cope

I was three years old and my mom was late driving me to kindergarten. (As a December birthday I was often the youngest in my class). Recalling this memory felt like watching a movie someone had filmed. I could see my mom come flying around the circle driveway of my elementary school in our minivan and slamming on the brakes right in front of the side entrance to my kindergarten classroom (in reality, she could have driven up at a perfectly normal speed, but this is how I remember it). Then she is out of the car and I am out of the car and we are standing next to the car with the car's side door open and I am having a meltdown. In the memory, on the outside I don't look like I am having a meltdown, but I can feel my mother's hand around my little arm. The energy inside of me is coursing through me and I feel panic and fear and anger and anxiety and confusion and sadness and shame. I can feel my mother holding me up by my arm, although from the outside it looks normal, like she simply has her hand on my arm, she is not dragging me, she is not pulling me out of the car, but it *feels like* she is doing both.

She is bent over, looking my three-year-old self in the eye. I can't hear what she is saying. I think she may be trying to console me but mostly I feel her not knowing what to do with all my feelings. She is trying to get me to come inside to kindergarten. Ms. Burton (my teacher) will be so happy to see me, she says. I don't care. I am late. I am bad. I am not okay. *I am a mess and I cannot let anyone, especially Ms. Burton, see me like this.*

I have no memory of what happens next. I don't remember if I went into class. I think maybe I did and Ms. Burton was happy to see me and eventually I was fine. But what I do remember is (1) feeling all the feelings, (2) being paralyzed by them and not knowing how to navigate myself through them, and (3) my mom being at a loss for helping me navigate them, too.

My feelings were too much. Too much for me. Too much for my mom. Too much for Ms. Burton. Too much for the world. Too many feelings were bad. I had too many feelings. I am bad because I have too many feelings. This is my struggle. This is my curse. This is how it will always be. This is the story my little three-year-old self told herself that day and this is the story I told myself for the next three decades. No wonder I didn't want to tell this story to my wife during a five-hour car ride on the way to see her family.

It is amazing how I could both pretend this was not my story and have it be one of my "defining stories" at the same time. I learned very early on that it was not okay to feel all my feelings. In this, I am not unique. I am fairly certain my mom learned a similar lesson as a young girl. And probably her mother before her and her mother before her. Feelings are powerful and women and girls are taught to equate that power with danger. In response we do whatever we have to do to mitigate the danger to ourselves and to others.

My mom learned to say that, "everything was fine." She learned to make everything *be fine,* for herself and for everyone around her. And because that was the way she coped, it was *not* the way I coped. We strictly adhered to the universal rule of mothers and daughters – *whatever your mother does you must do the exact opposite.* Since she coped by somehow managing to feel nothing (which, I know is absolutely not true, but that was what my teen-age-self believed) then I would feel *everything.* If she was fine then I was *not fine!*

Like every girl, I quickly learned what feelings were and were not acceptable in my family, meaning which ones got the response I desired and which did not. I often felt sad but sadness did not get the same reaction, i.e., attention. What got attention? Anger! I played up my anger every chance I got. Once my hormones kicked in it was open season. To this day I will still randomly call up my mom and apologize for the years 1995–2000.

I was a bi*ch. I did not know what else to do. *I had all these feelings* and the only way I knew how to deal with them, or move them through my body, was to rage. In hindsight, I was actually a genius, because feelings stuck in our bodies cause all kinds of sh*t to happen. We *need* to move our feelings through us to process them. Of course, it would have been better if I had had the tools to direct all the anger and rage I felt at a pillow or punching bag rather than my mother. I never hit her but I did hit the wall once. And a window. It broke and I got five stitches. I still have the scar.

Feeling Is Healing

Human beings have feelings, lots and lots of feelings, and we have precious few tools for doing constructive things with them, like listening to them and interpreting the messages they are trying to tell us. Most of what we have are dulling mechanisms and bypass systems that help us to survive but don't do much to help us thrive.

Thank freaking God/Goddess/Source/All That Is Good and Holy for the people in the world who have made it their life's mission to help others know and understand their feelings. Two people who have helped me immensely are Bill Kondrath and Regena Thomashauer. Read everything they have written. *Seriously*. Go study with them if you can. I want to be there if and when they ever meet. They are *very different* but the heart of their work is the same – *feel your feelings*.

When it comes to unlearning ways of being that are unhelpful and retraining ourselves to become healthy and whole, our feelings can and will take up a large focus of our attention. Feel your feelings. Write this on a hundred post-it notes and put it all over the places you live and work. Tattoo it on your forearm. Train yourself to say it to yourself whenever an uncomfortable emotion arises.

Your feelings are your number one superpower. I am not much of a comic book person but I do know that when a superhero first gets their superpowers they need to learn how to use them. Same with us and our feelings. Think of this as the part of your training in the art of feminine spiritual leadership where you enter "Feelings Country."

Imagine it is the size of Texas. You have all kinds of feelings about even entering Feelings Country. But you know that your desired destination lies on the other side. And the only way is through. There is no train to wholeness that goes around Feelings Country. You got to go in. Trust me, you will be okay.

In Feelings Country there are six counties, representing the six core emotions: sad, mad, scared, joyful, powerful, peaceful. You may want to immediately separate them into three "bad" counties and three "good" counties and plan your trip so you avoid going through sad, mad, and scared. *Do not to do that.* There are no good or bad emotions, just emotions. Also, it is not possible.

The "Take a Trip through Feelings Country" Tool:

- Think back over your childhood and remember which counties in Feelings Country you were allowed to visit, and which were you forbidden from visiting.
- How did you know which feelings counties were off limits?
- What kind of messages did you receive about your feelings?
- What is the story you were taught about your feelings that you have carried with you?
- As you have these memories, what feelings are stirred up in you about your childhood experiences?
- How do you feel about the messages you were given?

- How did the story you were told, or told yourself, about your feelings serve you and keep you safe?
- How might this story no longer be serving you?

Once you start to excavate these messages and stories from your unconscious or subconscious it can feel both unsettling and liberating – it is both. Some behavioral scientist will say things like, "thoughts are not facts" to help people realize not everything they think is necessarily true. You might have a thought like, "I am stupid." That thought is not necessarily true, it is just a thought. You might have that thought for a variety of reasons. Perhaps you have trained yourself to think, "I am stupid" whenever you do something you perceive to be a mistake. You may also have trained yourself to feel sadness or shame whenever you do something you perceive to be a mistake. That feeling of sadness or shame is not necessarily true or not true, it is simply your feeling. Your feelings can provide you with information, just as your thoughts can provide you with information. Growth happens when we can become aware of both our thoughts and our feelings and how they inform one another.

Our ability to feel is one of our greatest gifts. I am going to keep saying it until you believe me. Our feelings are constantly sending us messages, communicating to us information about our world – the world inside of us and the world outside of us. The thought always comes before the feeling. Those same thoughts and feelings may have been occurring automatically for years but once you are aware of them you can then pause, step back, and ask, "What thought did I have that precipitated that feeling?" or "What messages might my feelings be trying to communicate to me?

Emotional Intelligence and Affective Competence

At this point you are (hopefully) on board with the notion that paying attention to your feelings is an important part of being a person who is both self-aware and has compassion for herself. But you may still be wondering how an awareness of your feelings and the messages they give you has anything to do with being a bad*ss priest. I bet you have some idea. I also bet you intuitively believe they are deeply related. I am sure you would not have to think too long to come up with example after example of the disastrous effects a priest who is not emotionally self-aware can have on themselves and others. Lack of emotional competence (some call it emotional intelligence) can be catastrophic in ministerial settings, not to mention in relationships in general.

Often our unexamined feelings are what get in the way of doing the work God is calling us to do and being the people God is calling us to be. Being the church means doing the personal conversion work involved in embracing people who are different than we are and radically welcoming others the way Christ welcomes us. This work *begins* with paying attention to our feelings. The work of becoming aware of our feelings is not about shaming or blaming ourselves or others, but of engaging in a process of growth through compassion and love.

In his book *God's Tapestry: Understanding and Celebrating Difference*, Dr. William M. Kondrath talks about his experience working with people and congregations to be more inclusive, accepting of diversity, and building relationships across differences. He says,

> *"As long as I can remember, I have espoused a theology of God's all-inclusive love while at the same time struggling to deal (sic) the realities of sin, abuse, violence, and evil. The difficulties I continued to encounter in my own life and in leading communities of faith were not, however, so much on the rational level. My difficulties were more in how to make my beliefs operational or incarnate, how to walk the talk. And what I have discovered is that, for me and for many others, the stumbling block has been in my emotional or affective being – in my heart, not in my head."*

The work we are called is whole-self work – soul, spirit, mind, heart, body. We cannot leave out any part of ourselves and hope to be successful. Much of our training in facilitating personal and communal transformation has been limited to engaging people on cognitive and rational levels, while leaving the affective realm relatively untouched. Venturing into this realm might make you nervous. Sure, some ministers have used manipulative means for unsavory purpose – preying on people's emotions to sell them bad theology and win converts, or worse. But bad theology is bad theology and manipulation is manipulation. Engaging on a feeling level is not inherently manipulative – in fact, there are levels of healing that can only be experienced through engaging and addressing what we feel.

Guidelines for Affective Competence

God created us as beings with the capacity to feel. Our lack of affective competence as leaders means we are missing an entire skill set – a spiritual gift set – for engaging and connecting with ourselves, each other, God, and all of creation! So many of our frustrations with institutional church dynamics have to do with how difficult it is to guide groups of people in working through conflict effectively and coming to an agreement, so the work can move forward. Bill Kondrath has something to say about this, too. "When you find yourself and the other person traipsing over the same intellectual ground for the third time, the issue is likely not intellectual but affective. Change happens only if we are emotionally ready." What if the church has simply not been emotionally ready for the work we are being called to do next? Then it is our job, as their leaders, to help them get ready! And we can't help them get ready, or lead them in doing the work of getting ready, unless we are also engaged in that same ongoing work ourselves.

So how do we become affectively competent? How do we feel all our feelings and become bad*ss experts at deciphering their meanings? How do we train others to do this work, too? A fantastic organization called VISIONS Inc. has created a set of guidelines that I highly recommend adopting for your own personal use *and* teaching to your people for just these purposes. Here they are:

The "VISIONS Guidelines" Tool:

- "Try on"
- It's okay to disagree
- It is not okay to blame, shame or attack yourself or others
- Practice confidentially
- Practice "self-focus"
- Practice "both/and" thinking
- Notice both process and content
- Be aware of intent and impact
- Take 100 percent responsibility for one's own learning
- It is okay to be messy

These guidelines are genius. Some of them are self-explanatory, like, "It's okay to disagree" or "practice confidentiality." The others need a bit more explanation.

"Try on" refers to the practice of suspending judgement and opening ourselves to a new perspective. Just like trying on a new pair of shoes, the practice of "trying on" a new idea or concept or even relationship does not mean you have accepted that idea forever – just like you do not have to buy that new pair of shoes! But in order to see how it feels you have to try it on and walk around in it for a bit, then if you decide it is not for you, you can take it off. Like the exercise of "walking a mile in another person's shoes," when you try on a new perspective you get a feel for what it is like, as best you can. Being willing to try on a new behavior or viewpoint means being willing to suspend judgment and open yourself to learning something new. Trying on new

understandings and ways of being allows us to practice our role as co-creators with God, for trying on something new ultimately produces something new in us.

It is okay to disagree. When people know it is *not okay* to disagree they do not show up as their full selves because they know it is not safe. Huge swaths of life become off-limits for conversation or engagement when the spoken or unspoken norm is "it is not okay to disagree here." Like the old adage "never talk about politics or religion in polite company," this is a way to control the conversation and avoid difficult dialogue. Ultimately, prohibiting disagreements is impossible. It is human nature. Diversity is a part of human existence. Differing perspectives add greater depth; even conflicting perspectives. Better we acknowledge and accept it than suppress and reject.

Allowing for disagreement is an act of maturity. The same maturity recognizes there are disagreements in the Bible. For what it is worth, Jesus did a fair bit of talking about politics and religion, and he had public and private disagreements on both subjects as well. Making space to permit disagreements gives us the space we need in order to grow. There is no room for growth and transformation without it!

It is not okay to shame, blame, or attack yourself or others. It is amazing how people will behave in church in ways they would never dream of behaving anywhere else. This is where the commandment to love all gets twisted. Jesus loved and accepted all but he did not love or accept all behavior. He was very concerned with what was and was not ethical behavior. He also had a thing or two to say about not shaming or blaming – "he who would cast the first stone" and all that. It is *so much easier* to blame than to take responsibility for our own part in the interactions we have, including our *reactions*. It is also easier to shame others and ourselves because that is what most of us have learned to do. Shame has been used as a great motivator. It is very effective. It is not all that creative. And it is not loving. If we want to grow in wholeness and love we must intentionally practice choosing not to shame or blame ourselves or others.

Practice self-focus. Good old "I" statements. Before you dismiss this guideline as old hat, think about how easy it is *not* to pick up this tool in moments of conflict or strife. When you want to make your case it is easy to say things like, "people are saying" or "everyone thinks." Really? *Everyone?* No, not everyone. Sue and I. Sue and I think you need to stop running over the rhododendrons on your way out of Bible study. But Sue is not here right now, so really, I should just speak for myself. Ten times out of ten we should just speak for ourselves. This tool forces us to practice paying attention to our own feelings by asking us to name them. Here is a real-life tool for valuing the dignity of every human being. We value *ourselves* enough to speak for ourselves, and, in turn, we value others enough to listen to their own unique experience, which goes a long way toward building healthy relationships.

Practice both/and thinking. The patriarchal world culture is very dualistic and very oppositional. Underlying most either/or thinking is a better than/less than judgment. Most of us don't even know how pervasive either/or thinking is in our own perspectives until we start to practice trying on both/and thinking. Notice when you use the words "but" or "however" or the like and then try replacing them with "and" instead. Both/and thinking should come easy to us Christians – our savior is both *human and divine*. And it is still hard for us. Just watch. You and I are both *human and divine!* See how hard that is! This one is easier – we are all both saints and sinners. The more you practice, the more intuitive it becomes.

Be aware of intent and impact. Intent is the intention or motivation you have for saying or doing something. Impact is the consequence or effect what is said or done has on another person or persons. One's impact may or may not be what one intended. Awareness of this is huge. Both intent and impact are real and valid and being aware of intent and impact means being aware that you may be responsible for an impact that you did not intend. When that happens the helpful thing to do is to take responsibility for the impact you caused, even and maybe especially if it was unintentional. Humans are fallible. We mess up. We will never not mess up, at least not in this lifetime. Learning to be aware of our impact involves learning to use our superpower of feeling all our feelings – because impact usually has to do with feelings. For all his failings, it appears Paul may have been aware of the difference between his intent and impact: "For I do not do the good I want, but the evil I do not want is what I do" (Rom. 7:19). Oh Paul, I feel ya buddy. Awareness is the first step.

Take 100 percent responsibility for one's own learning. Each of us has areas in our lives where we have privilege and other areas in our lives where we lack privilege based on our membership in "target" or "non-target" groups. Target groups in this country are women, people of minority ethnicities, LGBTQA identities, non-English speakers, children and the elderly, folks who are differently abled, etc. Non-target groups are the groups that you can be a part of and not expect to be targeted for – being male, white, straight, able-bodied, an English speaker; you get the picture. Taking 100 percent responsibility for one's own learning means you do not expect persons who are members of target groups to teach you about what it is like to be a member of a target group or to teach you about your own privilege as member of the non-target group. This. Is. Not. Their. Job. It is your job to learn. It is your job to listen. It is your job to ask questions and receive whatever response you get. Sometimes that response may be gracious. Sometimes that response may be, "f*ck off." You are responsible for your own learning and this is part of the learning. As Bill Kondrath says, "Taking 100 percent responsibility for my own learning means not expecting others to do my work for me." Trust that the Spirit of God is guiding us all into all truth. While the truth is a long and winding road, we will know the truth and the truth will set us free... eventually.

It is okay to be messy. There is freedom in the mess. When doing difficult work, sometimes all you can manage to do is sit in the sh*t of it all, metaphorically of course. At the Slate

Project we once had a twenty-minute conversation about the theological and ecclesiological merits of "sitting in the sh*t." When you start to uncover hidden and unconscious behaviors and you start to realize how screwed up we all actually are, it can be tempting to dump it all in the proverbial trash, wash our hands, and be done with it. That is not the work. The work takes time. The work takes work. The work takes getting really familiar with our mess so we don't end up right back here in the exact same mess tomorrow. Tomorrow's mess will be slightly different. It is okay to feel uncomfortable. Feeling comfortable with discomfort is a super-superpower. That is some high-level feminine spiritual leadership right there.

Say ouch. Now that we are practicing feeling all our feelings, we can start to introduce methods for engaging with those feelings in different situations and circumstances. While we want to be honest with ourselves about what we are feeling when we feel it, and acknowledge it is okay to be messy, we also need to practice creating containers for ourselves where we can feel and deal with these emotions in helpful ways. When you start to practice self-focus and increase your awareness of both your feelings and the feelings of others, you are going to notice how often we use shaming, blaming, and attacking in our everyday lives. It is important to practice stopping those behaviors in their tracks, even if you don't know what to do next. Awareness is key, right? One way to do that is to literally say "ouch," out loud, when someone shames you. If it hurts, say ouch.

We all want to feel safe. We all want relationships with people we can trust. We all want to feel like we can be honest with ourselves and others. This is what feminine spiritual leadership looks like. It doesn't just happen, it takes work and practice and a lot of tools. The VISIONS guidelines are some of the best tools I have found for communicating, particularly across differences, which let's face it, whenever you are communicating with another human being you are communicating across differences. The more you hone your superpower of feeling, the more you will realize that in so many ways we all feel the same things, and in so many ways our feelings are completely unique. Talk about bad*ss.

CHAPTER 9

The Wisdom of Your Body

———◆———

"This is your body, your greatest gift, pregnant with wisdom you do not hear, grief you thought was forgotten, and joy you have never known."

– MARION WOODMAN, COMING HOME TO MYSELF

Our Bodies Our Selves

I have lived most of my life in my head. My relationship with my body has generally been tumultuous. Just like I made a choice at some point not to put my continued attention on negative experiences in the past, at some point I decided the attention I was putting on my body was mostly negative. So, rather than choosing to put positive attention on my body (that seemed out of reach at that point) I decided the best course of action was to remove my attention from my body. If I couldn't say anything nice to my body, or think nice thoughts, then I wouldn't say anything to my body at all. I would ignore it, as best I could.

In an interview shortly before her death, Carrie Fisher said something like, "My body is my brain bag. It is just the thing that gets my brain from here to there." I would imagine after decades of people commenting on her body

– its shape, its size, its weight and therefore, its value – she decided it was easier to dismiss her body completely that put up with that noise. To keep others from being able to assign value and worth to her based on their assessment of her body's attractiveness and therefore acceptability, she dismissed the idea that her body had any value, positive or negative. She decided her body was not what was important about her – her brain, what she thought, that was what was important about her. It's a self-protection mechanism many women are familiar with.

As I mentioned before, I have recently begun to practice reconnecting to my body as a means of exploring a deeper connection to divinity. Western and patriarchal cultures say that if we seek enlightenment we should seek to escape our bodies; our bodies are limitations to spiritual advancement. This is what I have spent most of my life believing. Even after being exposed to liberation theologies, feminist and womanist theologies, and queer theologies, I still could not, in practice, make the connection that if I wanted to show up as who I was, fully, that would necessarily include my body.

When I came to the end of the edge of the church, it was both a rock bottom and an opportunity for a whole new awakening. I knew I needed to reach out beyond the literal and figurative walls of the church to find a deeper connection and a greater capacity for transformation. I was at the point where I would try anything, *even connecting to my body,* to find a way forward! The teachers who came into my life at that moment have spent their lives dedicated to awakening the feminine divine within each and every woman. For them, a woman's relationship to her body is where her journey of self-love and self-acceptance starts.

In the past I had been resistant to "feminine" explorations of divinity and spirituality. I do not want to replace one binary expression with another – my goal is not to replace masculine divinity with feminine divinity. I am not interested in creating a "matriarchal" church where now the women are on the top of the hierarchy and the men are at the bottom. Ultimately, the goal is to move *beyond* binaries. Most of us are just beginning to understand that human sexuality and gender expression are much more fluid than we have previously been taught. Moving toward wholeness involves reclaiming parts of the whole that have been neglected and left out. The feminine has been neglected and devalued for millennia. In order to move forward and eventually beyond the binaries, we first need to experience healing and reclamation of our divine feminine.

The Feminine Face of God

Connecting to our divinity through what makes us feminine is sacred. Women have the power to create life in our bodies. As women we have the power to bleed, to regularly shed what is no longer needed and be made new. As women we are cyclically connected to the cycles of the earth, moon, stars, and planets. As women we have superpowers, unique spiritual gifts, that only we have. There is a reason we have been suppressed, there is a reason we are feared, there is a reason we have been called witches and burned alive – *because we are powerful*. Fear in the face of such power is a deadly force.

We have internalized much of that fear. We have internalized the hatred directed at our bodies, not just from our lifetimes – we carry inside of us our mother's mother's mother's mother's mother's fear of and hatred of their bodies. We carry this lineage of self-hate in our very cells.

What does this actually look like? Once I started to do awareness work around how my thoughts, feelings, and beliefs were connected to my body, I started to become aware of the pain in my neck, back, and shoulders in a new way. I have had horrible neck and shoulder pain for years. But when my awareness started to shift to include all the ways I have been taught to hate and fear my own body, I started to feel in a "sixth sense" kind of way, that this pain was not *just mine*. I suddenly became aware that the pain I was carrying was *generational pain*.

The scientific fields of epigenetics and quantum physics are making amazing discoveries about how our DNA can store memories of our ancestors and how trauma can be passed from one generation to another. It is possible the pain you experience in your body is not only your pain, but the pain of your mothers and grandmothers. New understandings of reality are challenging what "reasonable" people have believed for years and what we have dismissed as "non-sense." Yes, these things make no sense – no sense in terms of the limits of our five senses. But you know, dear reader, even in these human bodies, we have access to so much more when we pay attention to what our bodies know through our intuition.

The art of feminine spiritual leadership includes awareness of both what our body can know through our five senses and what our bodies know beyond those physical senses. We speak of it as a "gut feeling" but it is more than that. Again, it is beyond the both/and. To access more of reality, and more of our power, we must go through our bodies, not around them.

At this point even some of the leading neuroscientists and spiritual teachers get it wrong. The goal is not to become self-*less*. The goal is not to transcend yourself to the point where you have *no self*. The goal, spiritually speaking, is to connect to that which is greater than you, that is also *within you*. The goal is to *move through* your little self, your ego, your "I," to connect to The Self, The Source, The Thou, which is also The I. God is All in All, therefore the way to God is not to empty yourself or lose yourself, not to move away from but to move toward – more, deeper, fuller.

God is not an absence but a presence. It is not your job to get out of your own way in order to connect more deeply with God, but to step more fully into the way of God, which you are already in because you are alive. You are divine energy. You are made up of the same stuff that makes up all things, which is not separate from God. We step into the flow and move deeper into the flow through our bodies not apart from them.

There is no escaping the present moment and in this moment you are an expression of the divine energy existing in a human body. Rather than spending your life ignoring or running from this reality, why not embrace it to its fullest and see what incredible gifts await you in this body?

It will not last forever, but does that make it more or less beautiful, more or less special?

God Became Flesh and Dwelt Among Us

Things happened when Jesus became incarnate that did not happen and could not have happened any other way. If God became flesh in order to show us the way to truly live, why then are we trying to escape the flesh so we can follow Jesus? Shouldn't we follow him into and through his experience? Ah, but won't that lead to death on a cross? Yup. And resurrection. And new life. And the stuff we say we are all about. We can keep talking about resurrection and not living it and watch our church die anyway, or we can live it and die and get to the new life part. It's our choice.

Either way, Jesus says it is not going to be easy and it is going to hurt. But being miserable isn't easy either. Creating hell on earth for ourselves also hurts. A woman who hates her body is living in a type of hell – not exclusively of her own making, but she stays there of her own choosing. She may not realize she is choosing to stay or that she has a choice at all … until she meets another woman who has set herself free.

What does a woman who has set herself free look like? You can see it in the way she moves, the way she feels, the way she lives her truth. She knows going through the pain is the only way to get to the other side. She knows pushing through the pain is how we give birth to ourselves. She trusts there is always life on the other side, even when she can't see it. She knows she is the co-creator of her own existence.

How do you become this woman? You are already on our way. You have decided loving yourself and caring for yourself matters. You have decided to believe you are interconnected with all things, so therefore, caring for yourself is a vital aspect of caring for others. You have decided to approve of yourself, finding yourself right and believing you are enough. You have decided to approve of rather than disapprove of yourself. You have decided that your ability to feel is a gift, not a curse. And you have committed to learning how to use the superpowers you have been given in service to the world. Now is your chance to decide that you have been given this particular body for this particular journey for a reason and that reason is love. Choosing to love yourself means choosing to love your body. At this point you may feel a lot of resistance to this idea, because you are still literally addicted to the negative energy you put on your body. It is the only way you know how to be, but trust me, you can unlearn that and learn something new.

This Woman's Work Is to Love Her Body

Let's start with a simple yet profound tool to help us reconnect with our bodies by unlearning those patterns of self-hate and reestablishing patterns of self-love. It is called "Tune-In."

The "Tune-In, Turn-Over, Turn-On" Tool:

- Go online and find Katie Bush's song "This Woman's Work."
- Start the song.
- Take a deep breath.

- Close your eyes.
- As you listen to the music let it wash over you.
- Slowly begin to put your hands on your body.
- Gently run your hands over your arms, your chest, your hips. Just feel. Connect to your body.
- As you keep moving your hands over your body say: "I love you. I'm sorry. Please forgive me."
- Say this prayer to yourself as many times as you desire. Listen to the song as many times as you like.
- When you feel ready to finish say, "Thank you." Say "thank you" as many times as you need to.

We each need to re-train ourselves to love ourselves. While it is a process that doesn't happen overnight, the choice you just made to love yourself *will have an immediate effect*. Tuning in to your body will make you feel different. You will be different. In fact, you will never be the same person again. That is a promise. You have changed yourself and you have changed your reality.

Movement and touch are ancient tools of the feminine spiritual arts. Women have been dancing together in circles for centuries. Most of us don't do this regularly anymore, *but our bodies have not forgotten*. After just a few minutes of fully letting yourself go into the music, you will remember. Your body is a genius. She is exactly who you have created her to be with your thoughts, your feelings and your actions and these new tools will help you create her anew.

Move through Emotion
Let's take this to the next level with a full-on Dance Break

tool. On the show *Grey's Anatomy*, whenever Meredith and Cristina would feel frustrated or angry one of them would call for a dance break. That is basically what you are doing here, but with more gusto than they did. Meredith and Cristina never really danced so hard they got all their "stuckness" out. You can do better than that.

The "Dance Break" Tool:

- Rather than doing several shots of tequila to prepare for your dance break *a la* Meredith and Cristina, take a moment to identify the emotion(s) you are feeling.
- Take that feeling and then remember what it felt like *in your body* to be two years old and having a temper tantrum – this is the intensity you are going for.
- If you are feeling anger or rage, put on a song like "You Oughta Know" by Alanis Morissette or "Counting Bodies Like Sheep to the Rhythm of War Drums" by A Perfect Circle (this one is *intense)*.
- If you are feeling grief put on Macy Gray's cover of "Here Comes the Rain Again" or Disturbed's cover of "The Sound of Silence." (Covers seem to make really good grief songs. I don't know why.)
- Close your eyes. Take a deep breath. Let yourself *feel* the music.
- Then ... Lose. Your. Sh*t.
- Listen to as many songs as you need to until the feeling inside of you is no longer stuck but is moving. (The emotion should no longer be something that is happening to you, it is something you are moving through. There is a difference. If you don't feel it yet, play another song.)

- Crawl on the floor, beat on a cushion, push against the wall, scream (scream into a pillow if you are worried about the neighbors hearing).
- Return any furniture you may have knocked over to its upright position and rehydrate.

Excellent job. Now that you have gone deep into the cave and faced your demons, it is time to find your way out of the darkness and back into the light. The key to finding your way out of the darkness is going to seem a bit crazy at first. You may want to dismiss it as ridiculous. You may think you don't really need to use *this key*, surely there is some other key that works just as well. I'm here to tell you *there is no key like this one.*

This is the key the church does not want us to have. This key, in our hands, *changes everything.* This is the key you bring with you into the darkness because you know it is your ticket out. This is the key you reach for when everything seems wrong and all seems lost. This is the key, once you have it, that will bring everything you have learned in the art of feminine spiritual leadership into perfect harmony. Everything is about to make perfect sense – not to your patriarchal conditioned brain, but to your divine, feminine body. The key ... is *pleasure.*

CHAPTER 10

The Power of Pleasure

———— ◆ ————

"The absence of the feminine is the absence of pleasure."
– Regena Thomashauer

Going in the Swamp

I was in a room full of five hundred women who were stomping, screaming, and writhing on the floor while music blared. The room was dark, giving each of us a semblance of privacy even in the midst of the crowd. I closed my eyes and let it all go. An ancient, primal noise came from somewhere deep inside of me. I pounded my fists on the floor and pulled at my hair. Suddenly the music stopped and the wailing died down. The energy in the room was electric. My skin was buzzing. "Do you need more?" our teacher asked. "Yes!"

Regena Thomashauer was teaching us how to "swamp." Swamping is one of the core tools in the curriculum she teaches at the School of Womanly Arts. (She outlines this tool in her book *Pussy: A Reclamation.*) When I found myself at the end of the edge of the church and knew I needed more, I happened to come across a video created by this school advertising their Mastery program. The program was for women who wanted more – more power, more passion, more from their relationships, more from their careers, more from their lives, *more for themselves.* I had no idea what to expect, but I knew the women in that video had accessed something special, something holy, and I wanted it.

One of the things Thomashauer teaches women is how to regain access to their full emotional range. Women who have been trained to suppress their feelings (i.e., all women) can have a hard time accessing certain feelings like anger and rage. On some level, every woman is angry. If she is awake, she is angry. That is what living in a patriarchal culture does to women. It give us a sh*t ton to be furious about and then says, "Now swallow that anger, dear." When we shut ourselves off from our anger, rage, and grief we shut ourselves off from our creative powers. Thomashauer says that living in a patriarchal world culture woman are permitted to play about six of the eighty-eight keys on our emotional piano. To be a bad*ss priest and create a ministry and life you love, you must be able to play all eighty-eight of your keys.

For a long time I was terrified to express even a little bit of my rage because I was afraid I would get sucked down into an endless cave of anger and I would never be able to find my way out. Many women have this fear. After years and years of stuffing down our anger, we are terrified of just how deep it goes. We worry opening the door to our anger will be like opening Pandora's Box. What if we can't shut it again? We are just as terrified of our own anger and rage as everyone else is.

But the more we practice playing all eighty-eight keys and accessing every inch of our emotional range, the better we are able to harness the power of our feelings. Swamping is an excellent tool for this endeavor and guess what? You already know how to swamp! You practiced the first half of swamping with the Dance Break tool in the last chapter when you were moving through your grief and your rage.

Coming Out of the Dark

The crowd screamed back, "Yes!" Of course there was more to rage! Wouldn't there always be more? We were just getting started. Another song came on. This time I kept my eyes open and watched as the women around me used their bodies to express the rupture they felt in their souls. The music coursed through us as we stomped, kicked, jumped, and screamed our way through another song. We could have ended our swamp/dance break right here, like you did in the last chapter. This would be "level one." But we are way past level one. Plus, I promised I would give you the key out of the swamp.

The way a woman finds her way out of the darkness and back into the light is through connecting to the light within herself. What is the light? The light is joy, love, hope, grace, goodness, kindness. The light is what lights you up and turns you on. Yes, I mean *that kind of turn on*.

Here is what Regena says about turn on:

"The experience of one's own divinity is not an intellectual occurrence. It is not something someone else can give you. It is a bodily experience that – for a woman – is activated when she is turned on. Turn-on happens when she takes pleasure from her body, which is an experience that women have been

taught to avoid for the last 5,000 years. We've been held
hostage by a patriarchal culture that devalues turn-on and
uses women's erotic brilliance in service to the masculine.
Yet the erotic is where a woman's confidence lives, where her
power is sourced, where she connects to her deepest feelings
and longings."

Releasing the shame she has been taught to feel about her sexuality is the last frontier on a woman's journey toward loving and accepting herself, which undergirds her ability to be in healthy and whole relationships with herself, others, and all of creation. These are not small stakes. If you miss this step, something will always be missing, something will always feel not quite right because there will still be an essential part of yourself you have not accepted or been able to love. To become the fullest, most integrated versions of yourself you cannot orphan any parts of yourself, including your sexual self. Not only will you be unable to reach the state of wholeness you long for, you will be essentially cut off from a key element of your creative and spiritual power.

Women have been taught to fear and deny our erotic nature. Particularly if we want to be taken seriously as spiritual leaders, the patriarchy tells us in no uncertain terms, it is unacceptable to appear sexual in any way. Those of us who attempt to own our sexuality are shamed and looked down on, even by other women. As far as models for women who own their spirituality and their sexuality, there are precious few. Beyoncé? Madonna? Lady Gaga? They are revered by many as spiritual leaders and they certainly experience their fair share of criticism but technically they are not leading congregations. And they are completely dismissed by "serious spiritual people." Sure, yours and my vocational struggles are a bit different than their's, but accessing our erotic power has the capacity to up-level our vocational abilities and superpowers, the same way it does for these women! Don't believe me. Just ask Audre Lorde.

The Erotic as Power

What Thomashauer calls "turn-on," womanist theologian Audre Lorde calls "the erotic." In her seminal essay, *Uses of the Erotic: The Erotic as Power* Lorde writes:

"There are many kinds of power, used and unused, acknowledged or otherwise. The erotic is a resource within each of us that lies in a deeply female and spiritual plane, firmly rooted in the power of our unexpressed or unrecognized feeling. In order to perpetuate itself, every oppression must corrupt or distort those various sources of power within the culture of the oppressed that can provide energy for change. For women, this has meant a suppression of the erotic as a considered source of power and information within our lives. We have been taught to suspect this resource, vilified, abused, and devalued within western society. On the one hand, the superficially erotic has been encouraged as a sign of female inferiority; on the other hand, women have been made to suffer and to feel both contemptible and suspect by virtue of its existence."

I could spend the rest of my life unpacking this quote (I just might). But she's not done. She goes on to say:

"It is a short step from there to the false belief that only by the suppression of the erotic within our lives and consciousness can women be truly strong. But that strength is illusory, for it is fashioned within the context of male models of power. As women, we have come to distrust that power which rises from our deepest and non-rational knowledge. We have been warned against it all our lives by the male world, which values this depth of feeling enough to keep women around in order to exercise it in the service of men, but which fears this same depth too much to examine the possibilities of it within themselves."

If you can reclaim your turn-on, there is nothing you cannot reclaim. If you can connect to your pleasure, you can connect to your deepest desires. If you can connect to your deepest desires, you can connect to God's desire. Once we experience the depth of feeling we can access through our erotic nature, we know the extent of what we are capable of. And when a woman knows what she is capable of, it is unlikely she will accept anything less for herself.

Once we recognize the power of our erotic nature we must learn to integrate this aspect of ourselves into our practice of the feminine spiritual arts. But how? All the tools you have acquired up until this point are going to help you take this final step in your feminine spiritual leadership journey. The practices of finding yourself right, right where you are, and being comfortable with the uncomfortable and the unknown will help you sit with your resistance. Reframing your resistance will help you recognize the impact the patriarchal world culture has had on how you feel about your sexuality. The belief that your worth is non-negotiable translates to this area of your life as well – your sexuality is a part of who you are and it is just as loved by God as every other part of you.

Tapping into Turn-On

Another song came on, but this one was completely different in feeling and tone. It was raunchy. Instinctively my hips started to sway slowly from side to side. "Now, connect to your pleasure. Feel it in your body," came Regena's voice from the stage. Faster than my brain could switch gears, my body responded to the music. The rage still lingered and a new feeling was present. "Is this what she is talking about?" I thought to myself. I had never felt turn-on and rage at the same time before, but as I moved my body and ran my fingers through my hair I felt both energies move through me and *I was in complete control.* I was making my way out of the rage, out of the cave, back into the light.

The path from rupture to radiance is through connecting to that which is deepest inside of you – beyond your pain, past your grief, under your rage. No darkness can overcome *this light.* In the darkest night of the soul, in the deepest, murkiest swamp, it stays alive. Your power, your pleasure, your joy, your life force – the seat of your soul rests in your body and you can always find your way back to her, through your pleasure.

As a woman, maybe this all sounds really good to you. Liberating! A deep truth you have always known! Halleluiah! But how the heck do we make a theologically sound connection between the power of pleasure and creating our dream ministry? How are we going to sell this idea to the church? First of all, that is not our job. Our job is to be ourselves. Be ourselves, be ourselves, be ourselves. Love our sexy, radical, rockstar selves. We be the change. We don't convince anybody.

Any ministry that could qualify as our dream ministry should not only serve us, it should serve all and be in line with God's desire for us and all of creation. Once again, we can turn to the indomitable Audre Lorde for inspiration:

"For the erotic is not a question only of what we do; it is a question of how acutely and fully we can feel in the doing. Once we know the extent to which we are capable of feeling that sense of satisfaction and completion, we can then observe which of our various life endeavors bring us closest to that fullness. The aim of each thing which we do is to make our lives and the lives of our children richer and more possible. Within the celebration of the erotic in all our endeavors, my work becomes a conscious decision – a longed-for bed which I enter gratefully and from which I rise up empowered."

Pretty hot, right?

You may not have realized it, but every single element in the art of feminine spiritual leadership we have explored thus far is at its core a reclamation of the erotic. Every tool, every practice, every art-form we have engaged with has been for the means of achieving greater access to our creative power and our life force.

Remember when we talked in Chapter 2 about building the bridge from where we are to where we desire to go and how we would be building that bridge while we walked on it? Lorde would say the very bridge we are building is "formed by the erotic – the sensual – those physical, emotional, and psychic expressions of what is deepest and strongest and richest within each of us, being shared: the passions of love, in its deepest meanings." I can't imagine anything stronger to use to build a bridge.

Manifesting Your Desires

When my co-pastors and I were developing the Slate Project the general exercise we engaged in was imagining what could be possible if we had a clean slate for being the church. For those of us practicing the art of feminine spiritual leadership, I have phrased the question this way: What is your dream ministry? It is essentially the same question, because really, you do have a clean slate for being the church. You have everything you need to create a ministry that will bring you untold pleasure. You already are creating a version of yourself that vibrates at a higher frequency than most people. You already are dreaming your reality into being. It's quantum physics, baby. When we pray we put our desires and our intentions out into the universe, which does actually change things. I know, as priests, we are supposed to be believe that, but if we *really believed it* wouldn't we do it more often and with more vigor?

Remember at the beginning of the book when I told you not to worry if you didn't know *how* you were going to create your dream ministry? The real reason is, the *how* is not up to you. The *how* is out of your control. The *how* is the domain of the Spirit (a.k.a. God, Goddess, The One with Many Fabulous Names). When you are ready and open, She will give you the *what* download and *it will come to you as a desire.* You may have been getting *what* downloads all along but you didn't know to recognize them as desires!

Once you have the *what* and you have identified your desire, your job is to get to work dreaming, imagining, and praying about your desires. You believe in prayer right? You have even tried meditation, maybe? How about visualization? Good! That is what you are doing here. I call it "Manifesting Your Desires" but don't let that scare you. It's really just prayer.

The "Manifesting Your Desires" Tool:

The basis of this tool is to imagine yourself, in the future, as if the thing you want has already happened.

- Imagine it is five years from now and you are living your dream ministry. What are you doing? Where are you doing it? Who are you with? What has the last year been like? What is the best thing about your "current" ministry?
- Grab a journal and write all these things down or record them orally on your smartphone.
- If this is hard for you, pretend you are five years old playing church. What is your role at your imaginary church? Who else is there? What are you feeling? What is the

best thing that happened at church this year? Act it out!

- Again, write all these things down or record them on your smartphone.

Jesus said, "You will say to this mountain move and it will move." You have the power to move mountains with your mind. You have been given the power to "do even greater things than these." You have the power to create your own reality. The first place it happens is in your mind your imagination, your dreams. As Regena says, "When we open ourselves to desire, we open ourselves to being completely remade. A desire is the interface between you and that which is greater than you."

Writer and feminist Emma Goldman said, "If I can't dance, I don't want to be a part of your revolution." The patriarchy says because our world is so full of violence and oppression, we should not express any joy or pleasure. This only serves to keep us stuck in the cycle of doom and gloom.

There were years of my life I was convinced I did not know how to feel pleasure or joy. I believed I was incapable of it. I struggled with undiagnosed depression through most of high school. In college my ongoing battles with anxiety and depression fueled a search for answers and a quest for love I was convinced could only be found outside of myself. I was a prime target for a predatory professor (who also happened to be an ordained minister) to emotionally and sexually abuse. I didn't know about how power dynamics in relationships worked. I could not pray away my depression. Everything in the patriarchal world culture I was swimming in said I was wrong, I needed to be fixed,

I needed to be groomed by someone older, I needed a man to tell me who I was.

If only I had known it was okay to struggle, to ask for help, to trust myself. Maybe I would not have waited so long. I thought I had to find my way out of the darkness in order to feel joy. It was in the depth of darkness I realized I had to find a way to feel joy *right then and there* in order to find my way through. As women we intuitively know rapture and rupture can *coexist*. In fact, there is rarely one without the other. We have the innate capacity to experience and hold space for both rapture and rupture, our own and each other's, *at the same time.* This is another one of those things that may not make rational sense but it makes spiritual sense. It is a superpower; a feminine spiritual leadership art.

I realize shifting your relationship with pleasure from one based on guilt and secrecy to one based on divinity and your birthright as an erotic creature is a big transition to make. There will always be a choice between good and evil. Each of us has the capacity within us for great harm and great good. In order to face the darkness we need to know where the light dwells. Now you know, beyond a shadow of a doubt, that the light dwells in you. And nothing can overcome that light because it does not depend on external circumstances to exist.

We access that light through our pleasures. As Audre Lorde said, "Recognizing the power of the erotic within our lives can give us the energy to pursue genuine change within our world, rather than merely settling for a shift of characters in the same weary drama. For not only do we touch our most profoundly creative source, but we do that which is female and self-affirming in the face of a racist, patriarchal, and anti-erotic society."

As sisters and priests, we have been chosen for this time and place to change the church and change the world. The idealized self-made man, the lone ruler of the patriarchy has taken us as far as he can. Now, we need a tribe of women to pick up the torch and carry us into the future. May our pleasure be our guide.

CHAPTER 11

We Are Not Supposed to Do This Alone

———————◆◆———————

*"Open your heart, fling your hopes high and set your
dreams aloft. I am here to hold your hand."*

– MAYA ANGELOU

I've Got Your Back

A few years ago I stood up in a room of one hundred plus
Gen X and millennial clergy and said, "I need to know
you will have my back." As the week-long conference was
coming to a close, we were asked to name what it was we
needed from one another as we went forward. After days of
using open-space-technology to connect around common
interests and identify common struggles, we had come to
the point where many of us were itching to come up with
something we could *do* to address the shared problems we
were facing.

One of the problems that had come up for many of us
was the feeling we were fighting our battles alone. The fact
that our ministries felt comparable to battlegrounds was a
problem in and of itself! But many people spoke of feeling
isolated, particularly that they were not sure there were
other clergy in their geographical locations who would

be willing to stand with them or even behind them if they were to take public and prophetic stances in their communities. Too many of us had had the experience of standing up to speak the truth to power in love, and the resulting response from our clergy colleagues was either silence or actions of outright malice. The expression "thrown under the bus" came up *a lot*. So when the question was posed, "What do you need from the people in this room?" my desire was clear. I stood up and said, "I need to know you will have my back."

As I sat down, many people around the circle nodded and voiced their agreement. "Amen!" someone shouted. After a few seconds of silence someone at the other end of the room asked, "What would that look like?" I stood back up. I thought for a moment and looked within my soul for an answer. Finally, the answer came: "I honestly have no idea."

I really didn't. At that point I did not know how to describe the kind of actions that would have resulted in my feeling the support, knowing, loyalty, and fierce protection I was desiring from my colleagues. Five years later I now have a better idea of what it could look like for clergy to have each other's backs because I have experienced it. I also have a better understanding of what it does *not* look like, because I have paid more attention to identifying and naming the experiences when I have not felt supported.

Here are a few examples of what has *not* been helpful:

- A colleague I worked for taking an idea I had for a ministry and starting the program themselves without asking me first or including me.

- A person in a position of authority over me encouraging me to engage in a particular ministry they wanted to see happen. When I discerned it was not the right time for me to engage in this ministry in the way they wanted, they withdrew their energy and support for a project of mine, including promised funding, without discussing it with me.

- A person in a position of authority over me responded to my request that there be a period of discernment and intentional prayer permitted before I was asked to formulate a report that would have affected the ongoing mission and vision of a ministry I was co-creating, by saying, "We all know that is the way the Spirit works, but that is not the way the church works."

The thing about these incidents that was most upsetting was not just what was or was not done by the other person, it was the feeling the exchange left me with. When a colleague throws you under the bus, even unintentionally, it *feels* like being taken advantage of, tossed aside, or looked over. Those are the moments I wonder what any of this is for and wonder if I should quit the church and go work in a yoga studio. Except, as my wife likes to remind me, there are people and buses there, too.

What has kept me sane and able to keep at least one foot in the institutional church has been those colleagues who *have* had my back. The folks who walk their talk know it is all about loving God and loving each other, and at the end of the day, the rest of it is bullsh*t. It also helps that they call BS when they see it and get just as mad about it as I do (well, almost just as mad).

Here are just a few examples of what a colleague "having my back" has looked like:

- Allowing me space to vent when I needed to vent and not giving me advice or judging my experience, simply holding space for me.
- Noticing what I am gifted at and sharing that feedback with me, both when I asked for it and unsolicited.
- Giving me credit for my ideas and the work I have done.
- Affirming my experiences and telling me my feelings make sense.
- Asking me, "What can I do to support you?" or "What do you need from me right now?"

These examples may not sound like much, but they mean the world. When have you experienced both being thrown under the bus and a colleague "having your back"? Take a moment and make a list. Name the people who had your back and take a moment to say a prayer of thanksgiving for them. Maybe even drop them a note to say that you were thinking of them and how much you appreciate that time they had your back. It will be interesting to see if they even remember the incident!

Find Your People

I really, truly, 100 percent believe we are not supposed to do ministry alone. Yes, we were built for this, but we were built for it *together*. I wish I could wave a magic wand and spontaneously move around the resources for each priest and ministry to have at least one other co-pastor. Jesus knew what he was doing when he sent his disciples out two by two. It's not just that doing ministry alone is hard, or that it is better to have a companion, or that it is less isolating when you have another leader by your side. Ministry is not a solo event, period.

If your ministry context does not have the money to pay another person, you must find other leaders in your community to do this work with you. You need an inner circle. Even Jesus had one. Find the people who are going to go up on the mountain top with you. They won't be perfect. They are going to be human, just like you are human. They might even be the ones who betray you in the end – but if they are betraying you, then it is not the end. And here is the kicker – if you can get through those moments of betrayal, work through the tough sh*t, and get to the other side, then you will know you have someone you can build a ministry with. There will be tough times, it will get ugly, you will have fights, there will be difficult conversations. When things get tough, most people start updating their ministry profiles and looking for a new job. Trust me, the new job will have tough times and get ugly, there will be fights and difficult conversations there, too. If you can find people who will work through the conflict with you and go through the tough times by your side, *those are your people.*

The Wholehearted Are Brokenhearted

I truly believe there are some things, some elements of ministry we actually cannot do by ourselves. They usually involve (1) some type of healing and/or (2) figuring out what to do next. Some healing can only take place if it is witnessed. Have you ever had the experience of telling someone your deepest darkest secret and in the space of your telling, their hearing, and their holding you in that vulnerable space, you were healed? There are times when the experience of God's forgiveness is that concrete – it literally comes to us through another person.

One of the most heartbreaking moments of my life was when I confessed to my then girlfriend Heather a way in which I had betrayed her. She looked into my eyes, held me with her gaze, and said, "I forgive you." It that moment, it might as well have been God Herself looking into my eyes and saying, "I forgive you." In my experience of that moment, that is exactly what happened.

We can literally *be* the loving gaze of God for another person in such moments. When we lie to ourselves and tell ourselves we don't need anyone else to hear our story or witness our pain, we waste this precious gift. As Dr. Brené Brown says, our capacity for wholeheartedness is only as great as our capacity to be brokenhearted. One of the ways we try to protect ourselves is by keeping all our broken-heartedness in the dark, behind the curtain. This is *especially* true for clergy and for women.

Clergy have been taught it is okay to be the wounded healer – that our strengths come from the places we have been wounded. However, the places from which we lead and show up and are seen, *must be places we have healed.* There is some wisdom in this and there are also some huge problems. No, you do not want to bleed all over your congregation from your pulpit. No, you do not want to go into a pastoral situation and *unconsciously* try to get your needs met when the moment calls for you to hold space for another person's pain. No, you do not want to craft your leadership identity from a place of *victim*. That is not leading. Those are not healthy spiritual care practices for you or for your people. However, what many of us have been taught and what is reinforced among most clergy is that we cannot publicly show our pain while we are in the middle of it. We can *have* pain and we can *have* problems, we just need to go in the back and get our sh*t together (or at least be able to *present* like we have our sh*t together) before we come out, put on our robes, and be "the priest."

Here is the problem with this: even when people pretend like they have their sh*t together, they don't. I'm not just talking about fixing your makeup and doing the funeral because you have to because you are the priest and there is no one else to do it. I'm talking about pretending that your health is fine, even when you know something is clearly wrong, but telling yourself you don't have time to take care of yourself, because you have a church to lead. I'm talking about pretending like your marriage is fine and that you will get through this rough patch if you just put your head down and focus on your work because really that is what is most important. I'm talking about pretending like you don't have a drinking problem because you have it under control and telling your parish you need to take a month of to go to rehab would be mortifying and ruin your career, so instead you just keep going because it's really not that bad and you have responsibilities you just can't walk away from.

Pretending we are not in pain, just like every other human being on the planet, because we are the priest is a lie that is killing us and killing the church. We have internalized this lie told to us by the patriarchal church that we must hide our truth because certain parts of our truth cannot be seen by the people we serve. Why? Because then we can no longer run on the model of "Father knows best!" Any "weaknesses" or "short-comings" must stay in the dark. Any struggles we face must happen in private. If we appear not to be in control of ourselves we will lose control of our congregations. And we must maintain control.

This way of being literally kills people. In my former diocese one of our bishops was a "functioning" alcoholic. While many people later admitted to suspicions and concerns, no discernable actions were taken to support her or require her to seek treatment. Three days after Christmas, while driving high and drunk, she struck a bicyclist with her car and killed him. She is no longer a bishop, or a priest, and is currently serving a seven-year prison sentence. This was a woman I did not know well, but as a leader in our church, I looked up to her. Our church is more concerned with keeping up appearances than making it possible for its leaders to put our health and healing first.

The only way things are going to change is if we change them. Could there be a more important time to have one another's backs than when we are going through a personal crisis? Shouldn't the institution be interested in doing everything it can to support its clergy, including making sure they know it is okay to come forward when they are in trouble? More often than not, the messages we are given, either overtly or covertly, from those in power over us, is making sure we are very clear what punishment we will face if we get into trouble. When it comes to facing the challenges of life that come with being a human being, we are somehow supposed to be beyond or above such challenges. Or if we do face them, we better do it behind the curtain. Once we have been through recovery we can preach of our victories, but until then, "shhh!" The problem is it is ten times harder to get into recovery from a place of shame and secrecy – which is exactly the place we are claiming our priesthood demands we keep our problems.

The Find Your Accountability Tribe Tool:

It is likely you have already begun to use this tool out of necessity; now is the time to get intentional about it.

- Who are your people?
- Who are the people who have your back no matter what?
- Who are the people you reach out to when you are struggling because you know you can trust them?
- Who are the people you go to for advice because you admire the way they navigate their lives?
- Once you have identified these people, reach out to them and tell them you desire to form an "Accountability Tribe." Ultimately, you decide what this means. Have a conversation about expectations and getting everyone on board and agreed to how you are going to structure the group and what you are committing to for each other.

- Decide how often you are going to meet and communicate with one another. I have found it is not necessary to meet in person regularly to have a powerful and effective group. But you do want to "meet" regularly, either over the phone or video to keep in regular contact. I also highly recommend text chains – just keep the sound alerts turned off if your text chain includes people in different time zones. If you can, find some time to meet in person. While virtual relationships *are real,* embodied interactions allow for people to connect on a level that is not possible virtually. If all you can manage is an annual or biannual retreat together, make it happen!

You want your tribe to be a sacred container where you communicate freely, deeply, and effectively. The VISIONS guidelines and the Imago Dialogue are great tools for this which you can modify for your purposes. You could even covenant together to use the tools from this book like Finding Yourself Right, the Enoughness Mantra, Dance Breaks and even Swamping. I am a part of a group that has virtual "Swamp Dates" where we all set aside time and space to swamp together over zoom. The essential elements of a tribe are holding space for one another and witnessing one another. You will also want to determine exactly how you are going to hold one another accountable.

Sometimes we cannot see the hole we are in or that we are headed down a dangerous path. Your tribe are your sisters who are looking out for you. They know you which means they know your growing edges as well as your strengths. Ask one another to look out for places where you might have blinds spots and invite them to give you feedback. This is such a huge gift we can give one another. When we have each other's best interests at heart and only want the best for one another, we can give and receive feedback that may be difficult but necessary.

Any healing that involves the healing of shame needs light to take effect. Those truths need to be told to some other person. "Some other person" does not have to be your entire congregation in a sermon or a newsletter article. That person needs to be someone you trust, someone who has your back, someone who will hold space for your healing. Someone who, as Brené Brown says, has earned the right to hear your story.

We must be willing to take our ministries and our roles as priests seriously enough that we refuse to hide our pain from ourselves or from the people we need to let in in order to heal. The wounded healer has wounds. Some of them are scars, yes. Some of them are old wounds that have already been healed. But some of them are wounds we have not even experienced yet! We don't live our lives in a vacuum. We don't minster as separate beings from who we are every other moment of our lives. As long as we are living we are susceptible to wounding.

•For too long institutional churches have systematically practiced covering up wounds inflicted by its own clergy on people whose spiritual and emotional welfare they were responsible for and allowed predators to spread their poison throughout the church, unchecked and unrestricted. It is not unrelated that churches in which clergy are required to suppress and reject any healthy form of sexual identity or expression have experienced rampant sexual abuse by their clergy, which in turn has been covered up and ignored for decades.

The patriarchal church has tried to pretend its clergy are impervious to wounding and see vulnerability as a liability. Feminine spiritual leadership knows without a doubt that vulnerability is one of our greatest strengths. Wounds are a part of life; they need enough air and light and attention to heal or they will fester. Infection spreads. So does healing. It is our choice.

It Starts with Us

We need to do better. We need to *be better*. And it starts with us. How willing are you to do your own healing out loud so that others can benefit from your courage and your willingness to receive help when you need it? This is an area where an enormous amount of discernment is needed. Who has earned the right to be asked for their help? Who has shown they can hold space for you and witness you in your darkness? Who has proven they have nothing but your best interests at heart?

If we are going to be the feminine spiritual leaders who change the world and rock the church, we need a tribe of sister-priests to not only have our backs, but our fronts, sides, tops, and bottoms! We are on a mission. Right now this mission has enough energy and momentum to start a movement. A movement to transform the patriarchal church from what it has been into what God is calling it to be will take every single one of us doing the hard work of healing ourselves, supporting our sisters, and working together with God to heal the world.

This is no joke. Nothing about it will be easy. Much about it will be awesome. This will be our life's work, that will continue *beyond* our lifetimes. We are picking up the mantle of priestesses long dead, whose spirits are ready to guide us as we run like hell toward our freedom. Can you feel it? The energy is building. It is bigger than you, it is bigger than me, it is bigger than us.

The tools and technology from *The Art of Feminine Spiritual Leadership* are not to be practiced alone but within the sacred container of sisterhood. Together we are building a container for ourselves, a tribe we can come back to again and again for strength, support, and guidance. We need one another to train together, lead together, teach together. We need to pick one another up when we fall and hold one another when we fall apart. No woman ever needs to be fixed. What she needs is to be witnessed, held, and fiercely loved until she remembers how to fiercely love herself. That is what we do for one another. Find your tribe. Find your sisters. Sisterhood will be your greatest asset – more than a tool, it will be your home.

Becoming the Person You Are Meant to Be

---•---

*"Nothing is more surprising than the
new within ourselves"*

– Paul Tilich

When we began our journey together at the start of this book, we were in a place of dissatisfaction with our ministries, with the institutional church, with ourselves, with our lives. Where there is lack there is often longing and longing is where desire lives. By now you know that your desires are the keys to making your dreams come true. Your desires are not evil or sinful or bad. They are not to be avoided or repressed or ignored. They are to be embraced! Your desires are where God speaks to you – where your dreams and God's dreams co-mingle and conspire to meet the deep longings in the heart of the world.

The longings of our hearts are always deeper and truer than they first appear. You may have picked up this book looking for tools and resources for discerning whether to stay in your current ministry or take another job. You may have been looking for program tips to get more people to come to your church. You may have hoped I would share strategies for how to grow your ministry online. You may have been looking for a list of leadership characteristics to help take your career to the next level.

All of those things are great. But I promised you this book would help you be a bad*ss priest and create a ministry you love. To be a bad*ss priest you need to be yourself. And to be yourself you need to know who you are and you need to believe, with all your heart, that you are the sh*t. Otherwise you will never choose to be yourself. You will continue to be some other version of a priest based on some external indicators of who you should be. And if you do that you will never create a ministry you love.

Say you took a new job where you ran all the perfect programs, tripled the size of your congregation, developed a groundbreaking online ministry and made it to the top leadership tier of your denomination. Can you guarantee you would love it? Can you guarantee it would be your *dream come true?*

What would make it your dream come true? What would make it the ministry you were born to do? The only way to find your true vocational path – to be the priest no one else can be and to create the ministry no one else can create - is to follow your heart, follow *your* truth, follow your longings, follow your desires. Until you believe that God is *in* those desires you will resist them and you will resist your true calling. I care about you and the church too much to let that happen. That is why I have shared with you all the best tools and resources I have found for being bad*ss enough to follow your truth.

The patriarchal church needs a massive infusion of

feminine leadership to take us where we need to go. I haven't actually told you anything in this book that you didn't on some level already know. I just helped you claim it as feminine and gave you the permission to go all in. Now, the only thing left to do is give yourself permission.

The "Permission Slip" Tool:
(This one is from Brené Brown.)

- Get a post-it note or a piece of paper and something to write with.
- Write down, "I (name) give myself permission to..."
- Write down whatever it is that you are looking for permission to do, be, say, think or feel.
- Now you have permission. Post this where you can see it regularly until you don't need it anymore because now you *have it.*

The journey to trust yourself, just as you are, right where you are, is not a straight line. It is more like a spiral, with God at the center. Unlearning and undoing centuries of patriarchal conditioning that has told us if we want something it must be bad for us will be an ongoing process. Don't beat yourself up if you find these changes don't happen overnight or if you find yourself "right back where you started." In those moments, remind yourself you are not right back where you started – you are not the same person you were yesterday or even five minutes ago. Choose to have compassion for yourself and reach for a tool.

You have been co-creating your life with God all along. Now you are ready to "up-level" – go deeper into your truth, manifest your desires, co-create your dreams. You now have all the tools you need to take the next steps on your journey to loving yourself and being yourself.

In order to lead radical, world-changing, life-transforming churches, we need to know the communities we desire to create are possible because we have experienced them. Part of my longing and my desire in writing this book is to create a community of women spiritual leaders who have each other's backs. Just like our best sermons are the ones we preach to ourselves, the community we need is the community we are called to create.

There are answers to questions that cannot be found except for in the space between us. There is healing that cannot happen apart from being witnessed by one another. There is a future beckoning us that we can only create together – that we *get to create together!* When we connect, when we share, when we have conversations at four in the morning, our collective energy opens portals to other worlds, to energies and possibilities that did not and could not otherwise exist

Sonya Renee Taylor says, "There are times when our unflinching honesty, vulnerability, and empathy will create a transformative portal, an opening to a completely new way of living." My prayer is this book opens a portal for a community of women who are committed to loving and healing ourselves, so we can love and heal the world. This is what living the art of feminine spiritual leadership is all about. What a fantastic time to be alive and to be in ministry. I'm honored to have been on this leg of the journey with you and I *can't wait* to see where we go next!

Further Reading

- Braving the Wilderness: The Quest for True Belonging and the Courage to Stand Alone by Brené Brown
- Daring Greatly: How the Courage to Be Vulnerable Transforms the Way We Live, Love, Parent, and Lead by Brené Brown
- Rising Strong: How the Ability to Reset Transforms the Way We Live, Love, Parent, and Lead by Brené Brown
- Women Who Run with the Wolves: Myths and Stories of the Wild Woman Archetype by Clarissa Pinkola Estés
- Imago Relationship Therapy: Perspectives on Theory by Mo Therese Hannah and Wade Luque
- The Dance of the Dissident Daughter: A Woman's Journey from Christian Tradition to the Sacred Feminine by Sue Monk Kidd
- God's Tapestry Understanding and Celebrating Differences by William M. Kondrath
- Facing Feelings in Faith Communities by William M. Kondrath
- The Body Is Not an Apology: The Power of Radical Self-Love by Sonya Renee Taylor
- Pussy: A Reclamation by Regena Thomashauer

Acknowledgments

I've had three or four books rattling around inside of me for several years now, wanting to be written. If it were not for Angela Lauria and The Author Incubator, this book would not have gotten done when it did. Thank you to Ora North, Bethany Davis, and Norman Plotkin for your listening ears, helpful feedback, and wise guidance.

Thank you to Whitney Rice – my "Ideal Reader," whose passion, struggles, and desires I held in my heart as I wrote this book. I hope it speaks to you and, subsequently, many others.

To my colleagues and friends, especially April Stace, Ann Phelps, Lydia Bucklin, Cathy Boyd, Sherilyn Pearce, Jennifer Pedrick, Connie Reinhardt. Your love for the church and your critique of the church keep me sane and grounded.

To my seminary crew: Kathryn Reinhard, Whitney Rice, Lindsay Lunnum, Diana Carrol, Hillary Raining, Johanna Baker, Anna Doherty, Jennifer Zogg. FCA forever!

And finally, to my wife, Heather Goff. Thank you for being my person.

About the Author

THE REV. DR. SARA SHISLER GOFF is an Episcopal priest, school chaplain, mission developer, and spiritual coach.

Sara received her MDiv and STM from Yale Divinity School and Doctor of Ministry from Episcopal Divinity School, focusing on re-imagining the church for the twenty-first century. She has trained with Brené Brown and is a certified Daring Way facilitator. She has also studied extensively with Regena Thomashauer at the School of Womanly Arts.

Sara is the co-founder and former co-pastor of the Slate Project, an alternative Christian community rooted in the ancient, the arts, and the commitment to social justice.

She is the former Director of Communications and Ministry Development for Listening Hearts Ministries, a faith-based non-profit committed to teaching individuals and groups the practice of spiritual discernment.

She has been published in the *Journal of Religious Leadership* and has been interviewed by The Work of the People. In 2015–2016 she was a member of the final class of Beatitudes Society Fellows.

Sara lives with her wife on the island of Maui in Hawaii. You can follow Sara on Twitter at @revshiz and on her blog at **sarashislergoff.com.**

About Difference Press

Difference Press offers entrepreneurs, including life coaches, healers, consultants, and community leaders, a comprehensive solution to get their books written, published, and promoted. A boutique-style alternative to self-publishing, Difference Press boasts a fair and easy-to-understand profit structure, low-priced author copies, and author-friendly contract terms. Its founder, Dr. Angela Lauria, has been bringing to life the literary ventures of hundreds of authors-in-transformation since 1994.

LET'S MAKE A DIFFERENCE WITH YOUR BOOK
You've seen other people make a difference with a book. Now it's your turn. If you are ready to stop watching and start taking massive action, reach out.

"Yes, I'm ready!"

In a market where hundreds of thousands books are published every year and are never heard from again, all participants of The Author Incubator have bestsellers that are actively changing lives and making a difference.

"In two years we've created over 250 bestselling books in a row, 90% from first-time authors." We do this by selecting the highest quality and highest potential applicants for our future programs.

Our program doesn't just teach you how to write a book—our team of coaches, developmental editors, copy editors, art directors, and marketing experts incubate you from book idea to published bestseller, ensuring that the book you create can actually make a difference in the world. Then we give you the training you need to use your book to make the difference you want to make in the world, or to create a business out of serving your readers. If you have life-or world-changing ideas or services, a servant's heart, and the willingness to do what it REALLY takes to make a difference in the world with your book, go to http://theauthorincubator.com/apply/ to complete an application for the program today.

Other Books by Difference Press

Unleash Your Career Potential: 7 Steps to Living Your Dream

by Karla Blanco

The Energetics of Joy: Natural Rebalancing Secrets to Stop Stressing and Start Living the Life You Want by

Dr. Michelle Eggenberger

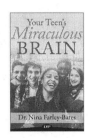

Your Teen's Miraculous Brain: Eight Essentials of Faith-Based and Neuroscience Informed Parenting

by Dr. Nina Farley-Bates

The Happiness Textbook: The Ultimate Manual for Mastering Law of Attraction

by Olivia Tiffin

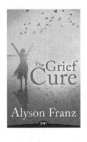

The Grief Cure: A Revolutionary Guide to Healing from the Loss of a Parent

by Alyson Franz

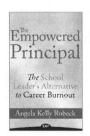

The Empowered Principal: The School Leader's Alternative to Career Burnout

by Angela Kelly Robeck

Competitive Advantage: Create Continuing Education That Is Profitable, Sustainable, and Impactful

by Tracy King

Parenting for Success: Raise Joyful, Fulfilled, and Effective Children

by Daniel Kingston

Thank You!

Well, my dear, we made it. It was quite a ride. And it's not over yet! Now you have a few more tools for your pink tool belt and more practices for being a bad*ss priest who loves her ministry and her life. I have every confidence that you are going to rock this sh*t – you have buried your old self and witnessed your resurrection, what can't you do!

I hope you noticed that, for me, this is not just a book. This is a movement of women, discovering who they truly are, who we have always been, learning to radically live and care for ourselves so we can facilitate the transformations God desires to bring about in and through us. My desire is to be a resource for you as you continue your journey. There is more work to be done together. And if you are ready to go off running by yourself, I bless you and I pray for you and the people you love, serve, and serve with every day.

If you want more, let's create more, together! I'm building a gathering place for our emerging tribe over at theartoffemininespiritualleadership.com. One of the things I am feeling called to do next is to invite small groups of women to join one another in doing this work together where we will work through the material covered in this book and go deeper into some of the practices, including practicing using the tools with one another. If this sounds like something you desire to be a part of send me an email at admin@sarashislergoff.com and we will connect.

I am beyond excited for you and proud of you. The church, the world, is blessed to have you. Thank you for showing up. Thank you for doing the work. Thank you for being you. Remember, the true art of feminine spiritual leadership is leading and loving as ourselves. Be fierce. Be a bad*ss. Be you. All my love, SSG.